ISBN 978-1-330-93682-5
PIBN 10123626

1 MONTH OF
FREE
READING

at

www.ForgottenBooks.com

By purchasing this book you are eligible for one month membership to ForgottenBooks.com, giving you unlimited access to our entire collection of over 1,000,000 titles via our web site and mobile apps.

To claim your free month visit:

www.forgottenbooks.com/free123626

English
Français
Deutsche
Italiano
Español
Português

www.forgottenbooks.com

Mythology Photography **Fiction**
Fishing Christianity **Art** Cooking
Essays Buddhism Freemasonry
Medicine **Biology** Music **Ancient**
Egypt Evolution Carpentry Physics
Dance Geology **Mathematics** Fitness
Shakespeare **Folklore** Yoga Marketing
Confidence Immortality Biographies
Poetry **Psychology** Witchcraft
Electronics Chemistry History **Law**
Accounting **Philosophy** Anthropology
Alchemy Drama Quantum Mechanics
Atheism Sexual Health **Ancient History**
Entrepreneurship Languages Sport
Paleontology Needlework Islam
Metaphysics Investment Archaeology
Parenting Statistics Criminology
Motivational

MEMOIRS OF CHRISTINA,

QUEEN OF SWEDEN.

VOL. II.

MEMOIRS OF CHRISTINA,

QUEEN OF SWEDEN.

BY

HENRY WOODHEAD.

IN TWO VOLUMES.

VOL. II.

LONDON:

HURST AND BLACKETT, PUBLISHERS,

SUCCESSORS TO HENRY COLBURN,

13, GREAT MARLBOROUGH STREET.

1863.

DALZIEL BROTHERS, CAMDEN PRESS, LONDON.

CONTENTS OF VOL. II.

CHAPTER I.

CHAPTER II.

CHAPTER III.

CHAPTER IV.

CHAPTER V.

MEMOIRS OF CHRISTINA,

QUEEN OF SWEDEN.

CHAPTER I.

Salmasius at the Swedish Court—His Controversy with Milton—Milton's Eulogy of Christina—Enmity of Salmasius to Grotius—Vossius—Anecdotes illustrative of his Conduct and Character—The Two Astrologers—The Queen's Treatment of a Scurrilous Poet—The Intolerance of the Lutheran Clergy restrained—Christina's Ready Appreciation of Literary Talent—Stiernhielm, John Paulinus, Rudbeck Bishop of Westerås, Olaus Rudbeck, Francenius, Sternbök, Sigfrid Forsius—Christina's Correspondence with Ménage, Scarron, and Claude Sarran—Position of Learned Foreigners in Sweden—Outrage on Boecler—Anecdote of Scuderie— Visit of Bochart and Huet to Stockholm—Practical Joke on Naudé and Meibom—Notice of Bourdelot, the Queen's Physician—Disgrace of Magnus de la Gardie.

SALMASIUS was one of the most celebrated scholars who was attracted to the Court of Sweden. He possessed the learning which might be expected from the friend of Casaubon and Scaliger; but it

does not appear that his influence was beneficial to
Christina, or that he won her esteem. Salmasius
had changed his religion in a contrary direction to
most of the learned men at this period, and had
become a Protestant, chiefly through the persua-
sion of Casaubon. His bluntness, or rather rude-
ness, was praised until it reached such a pitch as
to offend all his friends.

He was, at least, no respecter of persons, for
when requested by Richelieu to write his history,
he answered roughly that he did not know how to
flatter. He was engaged in quarrels with almost
every literary man with whom he came in contact,*
but his most famous antagonist was our own
Milton.

In 1649 he published his " Defensio Regis," the
object of which was to praise Charles the
First, and, of course, to blame the English
nation.

The task of answering him was committed to
Milton—a duty which, it must be confessed, was
not performed in the most temperate manner.

---

* 'Bayle says :—" On eut dit, qu'il avait posé son trône
sur un monceau de pierres, afin d'eu jetter sur tous les pas-
sans." '—Tome II., p. 205.

Hobbes, whose predilections were on the royal side, read both these productions, and said that he could not tell whose language was the best, or whose arguments were the worst.

Milton not only condemned his opponent's arguments, but found fault with his grammar.

He accused Salmasius of false Latinity in the employment of the words " Persona Regis."* Salmasius probably felt the imputation on his style more keenly than any refutation of his arguments. He began a rejoinder, but died before it was finished, and Johnson says that Milton was flattered at the idea of having worried him to death.†

Milton's language hardly warrants this accusation, for he says, in his " Second Defence of the People of England :"—" But the conflict between me and Salmasius is now finally terminated by his death, and I will not write against the dead, nor will I reproach him with the loss of life, as he did me with the loss of sight ; though there are some who impute his death to the penetrating severity

---

* Milton's Prose Works, Vol. I., p. 8.—Locke had a controversy with Dr. Stillingfleet about the same work.

† Johnson's Lives of the Poets.—Milton.

of my strictures, which he rendered only the more sharp by his endeavours to resist."*

Salmasius excused himself when he first received an invitation to Sweden; but Christina was so captivated by his reputation as a scholar, that she continued to urge the request.

The compliments she used to the learned were sometimes as high-flown as those which they addressed to her; and she is reported to have told Salmasius that if he did not come to her, she should be obliged to go to him.†

He arrived at Stockholm in the summer of 1650, when the Queen gave him apartments in the palace, and treated him with a consideration that made him more overbearing than ever.

Although indulgent to his peculiarities, she could not always help laughing at his awkwardness, and on one occasion she called him the most learned of fools, on account of his fancy for interpreting dreams.‡ Much of the dislike and ridicule

---

* Milton, however, so far forgot his promise as to speak of Salmasius, a few pages after, as 'a grammatical louse.'

† Archenholtz, Vol. I., p. 232.

‡ Lettre de Vossius à Heinsius en 1653: apud Archenholtz.

which was attached to Salmasius was owing to a
shrew of a wife. Mrs. Salmasius boasted that her
husband was the most learned of nobles, and the
most noble of scholars.* She considered his
glory belonged to her, and esteemed herself the
Queen of Science. Her appreciation of her husband, however, did not make her treat him with
respect; she was, on the contrary, so domineering
towards him, that Christina said the patience
of Salmasius was even greater than his learning.†

She would not allow her husband to appear at
the Swedish Court in the modest and simple dress
worn by professors, but equipped him, after her
own fancy, in a buff leather waistcoat, scarlet
breeches, and an ash-coloured hat adorned with a
white feather.‡

Salmasius remained at Stockholm about a year,
when Christina yielded to the representations from
the heads of the University of Leyden, who told
her in high-flown language that they could no
more do without their professor than the world
could do without the sun. It appears that her

* Olivet, 'His. de l'Acad. Franç,' p. 395.
† D'Israeli, 'Cur. Lit.,' p. 67.
‡ Huet's 'Memoirs,' p. 195.

admiration for the scholar had diminished by this
time, and the following anecdote, which is not very
creditable to the Queen or to the Professor, shows
that she could not have had much respect for
him.

He had an illness while in Stockholm, and the
Queen, consulting her good nature more than her
dignity, went to see the sick man.

As she entered the room, he made some pretence
of hiding a book which he was reading, but which
she insisted on seeing. It was one almost unrivalled for coarseness, even at that time, called
" Le Moyen de Parvenir."

Christina opened the book, and obliged her
favourite attendant, the beautiful Ebba Sparre, to
read a passage aloud. The poor girl blushed and
hesitated, but finally obeyed, to the great amusement of the Queen and the old reprobate, then
sixty-two years of age, who indulged in fits of
laughter. It is not a little curious that Huet,
Bishop of Avranches, a man of great learning, who
professed strictness and even sanctity of life,
relates this story as an excellent joke.*

* Huet's 'Memoirs,' p. 196.

It is certain that the favour Salmasius was in, declined before he left Sweden. Milton's "Defence of the People of England" appeared in answer to his attack, and Christina is said to have praised the work of the great Englishman to Salmasius himself. This must have been galling to him, for although Milton's "Defence" contains many grand and eloquent passages, it is often disfigured by virulent personal abuse of his adversary, whose character and motives are represented as infamous.

Christina could not have read Milton's "Defence" without admiration, for noble passages occur in it which are scarcely inferior to those in "Paradise Lost."

In one part he notices the ungenerous and cruel attacks of his adversary, who reproached him on account of his blindness, and compared him to a cyclops, "a monster huge and hideous, void of sight."

Milton says, "If the choice were necessary, I would prefer my blindness to yours: yours is a cloud spread over the mind, which darkens both the light of reason and of conscience; mine keeps from my view only the coloured surfaces of things, while it leaves me at liberty to contemplate the beauty and stability of virtue and of truth.

" How many things there are besides, which I would not willingly see, how many which I must see against my will, and how few which I feel any anxiety to see! There is, as the Apostle has remarked, a way to strength through weakness.

" Let me then be the most feeble creature alive, as long as that feebleness serves to invigorate the energies of my rational and immortal spirit; as long as in that obscurity in which I am enveloped, the light of the Divine presence more clearly shines; then, in proportion as I am weak, I shall be invincibly strong—and in proportion as I am blind, I shall more clearly see. Oh! that I may be thus perfected by feebleness, and irradiated by obscurity!

" And, indeed, in my blindness, I enjoy in no inconsiderable degree the favour of the Deity, who regards me with more tenderness and compassion as I am able to behold nothing but himself. For the Divine law not only shields me from injury, but almost renders me too sacred to attack—not, indeed, so much from the privation of my sight, as from the overshadowing of those heavenly wings which seem to have occasioned this obscurity, and which, when occasioned, he is wont to illuminate with an interior light, more precious and more pure."

Milton's mind, at this time, was brooding over his immortal "Paradise Lost," and who shall say that he boasted unduly of that "interior light" of which he must have been conscious.

To quote such passages alone, however, would not give a fair impression of Milton's work, although it is less pleasing to quote parts which show both violence and injustice. He says in one place, "What school-boy, what little insignificant monk, could not have made a more elegant speech for the King, and in better Latin, than this royal advocate has done?" Again, he says, perhaps with more truth than modesty, "O flowers! that such a witless, senseless bawler, one that was born but to spoil or transcribe good authors, should think himself able to write anything of his own that will reach posterity, whom, together with his frivolous scribbles, the very next age will bury in oblivion, unless this defence of the King may be beholden to the answer I give to it, for being looked into now and then."

Even the title of his enemy's production did not escape Milton's sarcasm—" A Royal Defence for Charles the First to Charles the Second."*

He says "that Salmasius has neither modesty nor understanding, nor any other requisite qualification, but sauciness, and a little grammar only."

Although the " Defence of the People" was interspersed with tolerably strong invectives, it is worked up to a climax at the end, where Salmasius is compared to Judas Iscariot, and is assured that a place awaits him in the same region of torment with the arch-traitor.

A more pleasing part, and one more pertinent to my subject, is Milton's eulogy of Christina. His prepossessions were not in favour of royalty. He wanted neither pensions, gold chains, nor Court favour. He praised her because he believed she deserved praise. It is remarkable that two of the warmest panegyrics on Christina came from two men most eminent in their age for virtue and genius, although their talents and opinions were generally opposed — Blaise Pascal and John

* Defensio Regia pro Car: Primo, ad Car : Secundum.

Milton. Pascal's address to her has already been quoted. That of Milton is interesting as an evi-dence of the consideration and esteem which existed between the ardent Republican and the legitimate Sovereign.

After speaking of Salmasius' work, he goes on to say, " But your penetrating mind, O Serene Queen of Sweden! soon detected his imposture; and, with a magnanimity almost above human, you taught Sovereigns and the world to prefer truth to the interested clamours of faction.

" How happy am I beyond my utmost expecta-tions—for to the praise of eloquence, except as far as eloquence consists in the force of truth, I lay no claim—that, when the critical exigencies of my country demanded that I should undertake the arduous and invidious task of impugning the rights of kings, I should meet with so illustrious, so truly royal an evidence to my integrity, and to the truth that I had not written a word against kings, but only against tyrants, the spots and the pests of royalty. But you, O Augusta! possessed not only so much magnanimity, but were so irradiated by the glorious beams of wisdom and of virtue, that you not only read with patience, with incredible impartiality, with a serene complacency of countenance, what might seem to be levelled against your rights and dignity; but expressed such an opinion of the defender of these rights— Salmasius—as may well be considered an adjudication of the palm of victory to his opponent.

" You, O Queen ! will for ever be the object of my homage, my veneration, and my love; for it was your greatness of soul, so honourable to yourself, and so auspicious to me, which served to efface the unfavourable impression against me at other courts, and to rescue me from the evil surmises of other sovereigns. What a high and favourable opinion must foreigners conceive, and your own subjects for ever entertain, of your impartiality and justice, when, in a matter which so nearly interested the fate of sovereigns and the rights of your crown, they saw you sit down to the discussion with as much equanimity and composure as you would to determine a dispute between two private individuals. It excites our astonishment to see a force of intellect so truly divine, a particle of celestial flame so resplendently pure in a region so remote; of which an atmosphere so darkened with clouds, and so chilled with frosts, could not extinguish the light, nor repress the operations. The rocky and barren soil, which is often · as unfavourable to the growth of genius as of plants, has not impeded the maturation of your faculties ; and that country, so rich in metallic ore, which appears like a cruel step-mother to others, seems to have been a fostering parent to you ; and, after the most strenuous attempts, to have at last produced a progeny of pure gold. . . . . . . She herself seems the least conscious of her own attributes of sovereignty, and her thoughts are always fixed on something greater and more sublime than the glitter of a crown. She may, if such is the fatality of the Swedish nation, abdicate the sovereignty, but she can never lay aside the queen, for her reign has proved that she is fit to govern, not only Sweden, but the world."

If Salmasius was rather hardly used by Milton, he was treated with silent and dignified contempt by another great man whom he attacked, but whose temper was too placid to let such an adversary divert him from his studies.

Salmasius had always professed himself the friend of Grotius, but when the book " De Jure Belli et Pacis " appeared, he abused it violently,

although at the same time he made free use of it
in his own works.*

When Grotius became ambassador at Paris,
Salmasius again professed friendship for him, nor
did the great man show any signs of resentment
at his former impertinence.

Salmasius opposed the attempts of Grotius to
bring about a reconciliation between the different
churches.†

A bitter hatred for his noble opponent supplied
the place of argument, but his most malignant
attacks were reserved until after the death of
Grotius. Then Salmasius did all in his power to
blacken the memory of the illustrious patriot and
philosopher. The spitefulness of his attacks was
equalled by their impotence, and the fame of
Grotius stood out the brighter the more it was
discussed.

Although Salmasius appears to have suffered in
the Queen's esteem, his learning covered a multitude of sins. She never amused herself with the

* Vie de Grotius, p. 242.
† 'In his book, "De Primatu Petri," he endeavoured to
prove that St. Peter had never been at Rome.'—Patineana, p.
14. Amsterdam, 1703.

squabbles of rival professors, but, on the contrary, often appeased their mutual enmity by an impartial recognition of their merits, and by a generous toleration of their faults.

Salmasius was dismissed with handsome presents, and with an annual pension, which, however, he only enjoyed two years before his death.

His widow, who had seldom obeyed him while he was alive, complied scrupulously after he was dead with the directions he had left, to destroy all his manuscript writings. The extent of the loss is uncertain; but, at least, these manuscripts might have cleared up the question, how far his reputation for learning was really deserved.

Christina wrote a very kind letter of condolence to the widow, but blamed her severely for her act of obedience. She said, " Are you so much the enemy of your own glory, and of the memory of the departed, that you have committed such a sacrilege?

" You have killed a second time one who ought to have been immortal."*

Salmasius was not the only visitor at Christina's

---

* Archenholtz, Vol. I., p. 233.

Court, whose sole recommendation was learning.
A man of somewhat similar character was Vossius,
whose lessons in Greek had annoyed Descartes.
He was a native of Leyden, and had become known
in the literary world at a very early age.   When
his father died Christina wished to purchase the
fine library which he left.   Young Vossius agreed
to sell it for 20,000 florins on condition that he
should remain in charge of it as the Queen's librarian with a salary of 5,000 florins.   He filled this
office so dishonestly that he not only re-acquired
his father's books, but a great many more
besides.   Christina also employed him to travel
and collect manuscripts.   Vossius made her pay
the most extravagant prices for these treasures,
and when her affairs fell into confusion, he appro-
priated many of his purchases.

Similarity of character did not produce any
friendship between Salmasius and Vossius.

When the learned Bochart arrived in Sweden,
Vossius was sent to be his guide, but suddenly
received orders from the Queen to leave Sweden
and not to show himself again until he had made
up a quarrel with Salmasius.   When, however,
his apology was ungraciously received by the

other, a part of the Queen's displeasure was laid on Salmasius.*

Vossius was afterwards patronized by Louis XIV., and by Charles II., who made him Canon of Windsor.

Some idea of what Charles thought requisite in a dignitary of the Church may be gathered from the following anecdote :—

Vossius one day told some wonderful stories about China, which he evidently believed himself. Charles turned to some one present and said, " Vossius is a strange person, he believes everything except the Bible."†

He published some extravagant stories about China in a work called " Various Observations." In this book he assigned fourteen millions of inhabitants to ancient Rome, and twenty millions to a city of modern China.‡

He also wrote a book in which he advocated the Chronology of the Septuagint in opposition to that of the Hebrew text. He went so far as to assert the divine inspiration of the seventy, at the same time

* Huet's Memoirs. P. 141.
† Catteau Calleville. Vol. I., p. 330.
‡ Huet's Memoirs. P. 164.

that with strange inconsistency he openly professed a disbelief in all Revelation.

The Canon of Windsor knew enough of his times and of the English Court, to discover that a little occasional dogmatism would make his infidelity respectable. He kept quiet possession of his Canonry until his death, which happened when he was in his 72nd year.

Christina renewed her intercourse with him after she left Sweden, and sent him some materials for writing her life. Vossius would not undertake the task, either from indolence or from distaste for the subject, but certainly not because he did not know how to flatter.

Whatever may be said of the indiscriminate favour Christina extended to literary men, she was seldom wrong as to the kind of estimation in which she held them.

Grotius, Descartes, and Gassendi, she regarded with unaffected reverence. Salmasius, Vossius, and many others she admired and rewarded for their brilliant qualities, but they occasionally received from her sharp and well-deserved checks.

Others, with less ability and assurance, were treated with a generous indulgence, calculated to develop their talents. She not only sheltered them from the injustice of rivals, but from the couse-quences of their own mistakes and follies. A certain Buræns had been physician to Gustavus Adolphus, and was esteemed a man of some learning.

In his old age he became addicted to astrology, and not content with vulgar fortune-telling, he predicted the fate of the whole world, which he said would be destroyed in 1647. A friend of his, named Wolimhaus, was inoculated with the same folly, but the calculations of the two seers did not exactly agree. Buræus was certain the catastrophe would take place in 1647, while his friend thought the world would last another year.

Buræus had already given away the greater part of his fortune, which he was convinced could be of no use to him. He staked the remainder of it against Wolimhaus, in support of his own opinion that the general destruction would occur in 1647, and not in 1648. When everything went on the same as usual in the former year, Wolimhaus claimed the forfeit. Buræus had enough sense left to refuse payment until the expiration of 1648, as he thought the error in his own calculations did not necessarily prove the correctness of his friend's prophecy. In 1649 the sun was as bright, and nature as fresh as ever : in fact the world had rather improved, for the desolating Thirty Years' War was at an end, but the respite would have been of little use to poor Buræus, who was reduced to destitution, if the Queen had not generously given the old man a small pension."*

Christina has been accused of believing in astrology herself, because she did not positively assert the absurdity of a doctrine which was then very generally believed. She said that the stars, for all she knew, might influence our destiny, but that for her part she put more faith in terrestial astrology.

This was far from the blind credulity which made Wallenstein consult the stars on all occasions, or even that which led Charles I. to call in an astrologer to decide on the most favourable moment for making his escape from Carisbrook Castle.

It cannot be said that inferior scribblers gained

---

* Svenska Historiska Anekdoter ock Kuriositeter. Stockholm, 1849.

from her merely by their flatteries a consideration which should only have been accorded to merit.

A poet of very little talent once wrote some most scurrilous verses on the occasion of the Queen raising a brave soldier to the rank of a nobleman. The most offensive lines were,

> " Te comitem Regni Reginæ gratia fecit,
> Ut comitem lecti posset habuere sui."

Shortly after the verses appeared, the poet to his great surprise received an invitation to dine at the Palace. After dinner the Queen played at cards with the newly-made nobleman. During an interval of the game, the Queen, in a marked manner, but as if addressing the officer, pronounced the words, " Te comitem Regni." The poet was in the greatest consternation, and wished himself a thousand miles away, but his terror was unbounded when she presently began again, and repeated the whole of the first line. He threw himself at her feet and begged for mercy. Christina, in reply, took a handful of ducats from the table and threw them to the abject slanderer, saying at the same time that a poet ought to have something to drink for his verses. Encouraged by such unexpected clemency, he extemporized another line,

"Eveniant tales o mihi sæpe dies."

But Christina now told him gravely that he would do better to be warned by his previous alarm, than to be elated by his present security.*

The orthodox clergy were greatly offended when Christina extended her favour to a learned Jewish Rabbi, Manassah Ben Israel. He dedicated to her a work called "Conciliador," the object of which was to reconcile apparently conflicting passages in Holy Scripture.†

She was not indifferent, however, to the reasonable claims of the Lutheran Clergy, and Oxenstiern even accused her of favouring that order too much.‡

If she had not restrained their intolerance, it would have equalled, if not surpassed, that of the Roman Catholics. Notwithstanding her care, some isolated acts of clerical tyranny occurred.

Thus, in February, 1651, a peasant in Worm-

* Svenska Anekdoter. Fahlun, 1840.
† Grauert, p. 397.
‡ Grauert, p. 329.

land, was condemned to death for speaking against the rector of his parish.*

The names of several literary men have been
* enumerated, whose labours created epochs in science and knowledge, and Christina's quick appreciation of their merits certainly hastened the period at which their works became generally known.

There were others whose reputation has hardly travelled beyond their own country, and these might never have been appreciated at all, but for Christina. Their names were so little known abroad, that she has often been reproached for slighting the native talent of Sweden.

One of the most respectable of these men for his learning and his amiable character, was Stiernhielm : he devoted himself to scientific pursuits, as well as to poetry. He introduced burning-glasses and microscopes into Sweden, and in return was accused of sorcery and atheism. Two of the witnesses against him were a peasant, whose beard he had singed, and a professor, to whom he had shown a flea through the microscope. However

‡ Svenska Historiska Anekdoter och Kuriositetur, p. 50.

absurd it may now seem, Stiernhielm was in real
danger, and might not have escaped the death
of a martyr but for the interference of Christina.

Every such interference, of course, transferred a
portion of the charge from its original object to
herself, and the accusation of atheism has been
noisily repeated by many who never took the
pains to investigate its origin.

Stiernhielm afterwards devoted himself to less
dangerous pursuits ; he wrote a work of considerable ability on mathematics, called " Archimedes
Reformatus," which he dedicated to Christina,*
and he published a poem called "Hercules,"
which was the first specimen of blank verse in
Sweden. He gained more favour with his countrymen by a philological work intended to prove
the antiquity of the Swedish language, but as his
patriotism induced him to say that it was more
ancient than the Hebrew, he was again brought
into collision with the clergy.†

* Archenholtz, p. 335.

† 'Stiernhielm held a public disputation at Upsala with
Terserus, in which he said that Adam was a Swedish name ;
that A signified *of*, and dam signified *dust*.'—Archenholtz,.
Catteau Calleville, p. 341.

' Stiernhielm at least could not complain that the Queen neglected native talent, for she made him munificent presents, protected him from his enemies, and finally ennobled him.

John Paulinus, son of the Archbishop, was a learned lawyer. He published a valuable edition of " Grotius de Jure Belli et Pacis," and he was also ennobled by Christina.

Rudbeck, Bishop of Westerås, wrote some learned theological works. Christina visited him in his last illness, and received from the dying man some good advice to be on her guard against flatterers.

His son, Olaus Rudbeck, was much more cele-brated. His fame rests chiefly on his discoveries in anatomy, and that of the lymphatic vessels has been considered as next in importance to the dis-covery of Harvey. Christina took great interest in his experiments, many of which were performed in her presence, and when a Danish physician named Bartolin claimed the honour of having found out the lymphatic vessels, Rudbeck was able to appeal to the Queen as an actual witness in his favour. She sent him to visit the chief schools of Germany and Holland, and he remained

some time at Leyden to complete his study of
natural history. On his return he established
the botanical garden of Upsala, which was afterwards increased by Linnæus. In 1753 the
Academy of Sciences at Upsala struck a medal
in his honour, and Linnæus paid him a suitable
homage in naming a new plant after him.*

After Christina's abdication he wrote a work
in which he displayed more learning than judgment, called "Atlantica. The object of it was
to prove that all nations derived their origin
from the North, and particularly from Sweden. According to Rudbeck, Sweden is the Atlantis of
which Plato spoke, and this idea gave the title to
his book.

Christina expressed admiration of his erudition,
but said she feared his trouble would not be
sufficiently rewarded in Sweden.

Rudbeck was fortunate enough to retain the
favour of three generations of princes. Gustavus Adolphus was his godfather, and many years
after Christina's abdication, Charles XI. continued
the favour which she had shown to him. On one

---

* Hallam, Vol. III., p. 220.   Bio. Un., Art. Rudbeck.

occasion the King came to Upsala, and the professor invited him to dinner. Charles promised to
come, and Rudbeck told him to be punctual at
twelve o'clock, which was then the fashionable
dinner hour of the Swedes. The King was
engaged about some important affairs, and did not
arrive until half-past twelve, when he found his
host quietly eating his dinner. Rudbeck got up
and said, " Did not you promise, Sire, that you
would come punctually at twelve, and see you are
half-an-hour late?" The King laughed heartily,
at the same time that he made all proper apolo-
gies, and they passed some hours in sociable conversation.*

Francenius published some useful medical works,
and by Christina's express desire he gave lectures
and performed dissections in the presence of his
pupils. Christina herself constantly attended the
more important examinations at the University of
Upsala, when the Archbishop Laurentius Stigzelius
used to preside, and she encouraged both professors

---

* Archenholtz, Vol. IV., p. 237.—The hours were getting
later, for when Whitelock was in Sweden, twenty years
before, the dinner hour was eleven.

and students by a lively sympathy as well as by handsome presents.

Stiernbök was highly esteemed by Christina for his works on jurisprudence. Gyldenstope laboured in the same field, and was ennobled by the Queen. His works on history and morals are still held in reputation.

Sigfrid Forsius wrote on physics and natural philosophy, and by the Queen's desire he wrote in Swedish instead of Latin, in order that his works might be more generally accessible.

Although she thus fostered the native talent of Sweden, she certainly did not allow it to monopolize her attention. Besides those learned foreigners who were persuaded to visit her court, there were many others with whom she corresponded.

She often received letters from Ménage, a literary gossip whose anecdotes are still amusing, and by him she was kept informed of all that took place in Paris.

She used to have a literary assembly at her palace every Thursday, and Ménage had a similar meeting at his house in Paris every Wednesday, and she told him that his "Mercurial" was the pattern of her "Jovial." He composed a poem in honor of the Minerva of the North, which does not appear to have had much merit.

Benserade was at this time highly esteemed in France as a poet and a wit; even Boileau praised his effusions, although they are now universally condemned as trivial and affected.

Christina was inclined to err on the side of indulgence. She carried on a commerce of compliments with Ménage, which would give an unfavourable opinion of her judgment, if a little satire did not sometimes appear through her praises. She rallied Benserade rather maliciously when he received the appointment of Ambassador to Sweden, but contrived to remain in Paris instead of performing his duty. She wrote to congratulate him on escaping from his mission to the frozen north. She told him that his delicate wit would have received a chill from the journey, and that he would have returned to Paris with an intellectual cold. Then she told him that his appearance in a Lapland dress would have been so attractive as to endanger the peace of all the old ladies in Paris.

Scarron, the husband of Madame de Maintenon, was another of these small luminaries. His come-

dies have long been disregarded, yet they were
once considered to have great merit. He possessed
in a high degree that talent for conversation for
which the French have long been celebrated. He
sent one of his comedies to Christina, with a dedication in which he compared her to Mæcenas. :—
" But the only advantage the Roman has over
your Majesty, is that of precedence in time. I
would venture to stake all my share of Parnassus
that your Majesty would have supplanted him as
the patron of letters, and would have driven him
to despair, as your father, the great Gustavus, would
have done with Augustus if they had contended for
the empire of the world."

There were many others for whom Christina
entertained feelings of great cordiality, although her
acquaintance with them was confined to correspondence.

Among these was Claude Sarran, Councillor of
the Parliament of Paris. He was one of those
men who, without himself making any important
contribution to literature, mixed much with literary
men, and was esteemed by them for his sound judgment and good taste. His learning gave weight to
his other good qualities, and he was in correspond-

ence with the greatest scholars of his time; with
Grotius, Freinshemius, Vossius and Salmasius.
He performed various services for Christina, and
amongst others negotiated the purchase of the
famous Library de Mêsmes. In a letter, dated
November, 1650, she expressed her obligations to
him in the most flattering manner. She says,—
"Since your politeness leads you to say that you
have given yourself to me, I will tell you that I
accept with joy your devotion, and with your permission, I intend to boast of it. I will exercise
the rights which you have given me, with the
discretion and reserve due to a man of your
merit. I will only be absolute in commanding you to change the name of my servant to
that of my friend."

The regard she expressed for him seems to have
been sincere, for after his death, when he could no
longer do her any service, she wrote a kind and
feeling letter of condolence to his widow, in which
she said, "I am so affected by the loss which you
have experienced, that at present I can do nothing
to console you beyond joining my grief to yours,
and lamenting with you, and with all good people,
a man of such rare merit."

The learned foreigners who settled in Sweden

laboured under great difficulties. The rude natives often showed disdain both for them and for their earning, and in return the foreign professors some-times avowed contempt for those whom they came to teach. This mutual ill-will once caused a serious riot in Upsala. A professor named Boecler, a native of Strasburg, held a chair in the Swedish University. He had probably often been irritated at the dulness or inattention of his pupils, for on one occasion when he was expounding a passage of Tacitus, he concluded abruptly, "I would say more if the leaden heads of the Swedes were able to understand it."

The explosion which followed this injudicious speech may easily be imagined. Whatever their heads might be, the students proved at least that their hands were heavy, by assaulting the Professor as he left the hall. Not satisfied with this violence, they broke the windows of his house, and during the night they fired musket shots into the room which he occupied. It does not appear from this incident that the Spartan discipline observed at the Swedish colleges was effectual in maintaining order, although scholars thirty years of age were subject to the rod the same as children.*

* Whitelock's Swedish Embassy. Vol. I., p. 190.

Christina was very angry at the outrage to Boecler; she wrote a letter to the Consistory on the 15th of March, 1650, in which she ordered them to examine the matter thoroughly, and to punish those concerned without any partiality. She added that she would hold the Consistory responsible if any connivance were shown.

Notwithstanding her protection, Boecler was so alarmed at the storm he had raised that he sent in his resignation. Christina allowed him to depart, but endeavoured to soothe his feelings by the present of 4000 écus, a gold chain, and the title of her historiographer.

Scuderie was another of those poets of whom posterity has not confirmed the favourable verdict of his contemporaries. He had himself a high opinion of the fame which his verses would ensure to his patrons. He says that Princes should not think him importunate, or suppose that his writings are inspired merely by his own individual interest. " No," he exclaims, " I am studious only of their glory, while I am careless of my own fortune."

From his conduct to Christina, it would appear that this disinterestedness was not altogether an empty boast. When about to publish his Alaric, which was to be dedicated to her, she offered him a gold chain with £500 if he would expunge the eulogiums he had bestowed on Count Magnus de la Gardie, who was then in disgrace with her. Scuderie answered that if the chain were as heavy as that mentioned in the history of the Incas, he would never destroy any altar on which he had once sacrificed.* It was to Christina's honour that, notwithstanding her resentment towards De la Gardie, she accepted the dedication without insisting on the obnoxious condition.

The learned Bochart, the Protestant minister at Caen, was a graver and more estimable man, who united vast erudition with an amiable and irreproachable character.

Christina corresponded with him for two years, and at last persuaded him to visit Stockholm. He was accompanied by his friend Huet, afterwards Bishop of Avranches, who was then a young man, and wrote a lively account of their visit to the Swedish Court. Although a staunch Roman Catholic, Huet did not display any bigotry. He spoke favourably of the Lutheran Clergy, said that

* Biographie Universelle.

they were very hospitable, and opened their doors to strangers without expecting any gain.

This liberality contrasted favourably with the conduct of the Dutch innkeepers on the road, who charged not only for a traveller's entertainment, but also for the noise he made.

"When we were reckoning with our host, he put down to our account the barking of our little dog, and the noisy laughs of our saucy valet; and upon our laughing still louder at the charge, and treating it as a joke, the landlord called in some peasants armed with axes, to enforce payment."*

Poor Huet also got into trouble at Copenhagen because he looked at the King through a pair of spectacles.

At last the travellers arrived in Sweden, and were treated with great distinction by Christina.

The aged divine became warmly attached to her, and his friends were angry that he one day so far forgot his dignity as to play with her at battledore and shuttlecock.

Another occasion of offence to his friends was that the Queen requested him to read her a chapter of his very learned work on " Sacred Geography,"

* Huet's Memoirs. P. 189.

but just as he was about to commence, her doctor, Bourdelot, came in, and, after feeling her pulse, recommended repose. Huet considered this a designed offence, and inveighed bitterly against Bourdelot. The doctor, however, appears to have been right, for Christina's health had been injured by excessive application, and he ordered that, for a time, all books should be kept from her sight. Both the learned Frenchmen appear to have thought that every other consideration should give place to them, and, so far from approving of the doctor's judicious orders, Huet says that through Bourdelot's instigation the venerable Bochart was not treated as he deserved, and that, through the same influence, Christina almost repented that she had ever learned anything.

Even Bochart spoke of Bourdelot with considerable acrimony, although he acknowledged his good offices in procuring for him some Arabic manuscripts, which were of great use in his book on "Sacred Geography."

Huet's unreasonableness on this occasion may be inferred not only from the probability that Christina really required repose, but also from his petulant complaints that the French did not meet with sufficient favour from the Queen, although the cry at her Court was that everything was monopolized by the French.

Huet did not lose his own time in Stockholm. He found some manuscripts of Origen's in the Queen's library, which, with her permission, he copied. He subsequently gained considerable credit by his edition of Origen's Commentaries.

It has not been suggested by any contemporary that Huet influenced Christina's religious opinions, and he appears to have had no idea of her leaning towards Catholic doctrines, for he even spoke of her as being desirous to propagate her own creed.* This is itself an evidence that he had frequent conversations with her on the subject, and it is not improbable that he contributed, in some degree, to prepare her mind for her change of faith.

Although his book concerning the weakness of human reason was not published for many years afterwards, it had long been his favourite method of supporting his Church, to invalidate all philosophical principles by sceptical arguments.† To a mind embued with such principles, a church which

* Huet's Memoirs, p. 160.
† Mosheim's 'Ecclesiastical History,' Vol. II., p. 455.

appeals only to faith must be preferable to a
church which professes to base its doctrines on
reason. Christina had already admitted the in-
completeness of all the philosophical systems she
had studied, when she said that " the old fooleries
were as good as the new," and her mind was
therefore just in the state to accept Huet's con-
clusions.

The Frenchman was probably misled by her
political conduct, when he said that Christina was
anxious to propagate her own religious opinions,
for she acted with energy and justice when the
French Government proposed to annul the religious
privileges of the German provinces which they
annexed at the peace of Westphalia. Christina
not only refused her consent to this, but threatened
that she would even interfere by force, to prevent
such an act of injustice. Before Huet left Sweden,
he had the bad taste to write some satirical verses
which reflected on the people in general. Christina read the verses patiently, but recommended
him not to publish them. The venerable Bochart
retained his regard for Christina to the last.

After his return to Caen, he heard some rumours
of her approaching abdication, and wrote on the

subject to Vossius. "My heart bleeds to think
that the Queen is about to deprive herself voluntarily of so many opportunities of doing good,
which, when once out of her power, will never return.

"She will repent a thousand times when it is too
late; if she had no other cause, the blame of the
world would be enough, as that is always ready to
fasten itself on the great, when any specious pretext occurs."

Bochart's industry did not diminish, notwithstanding his advanced age, and he died suddenly
while addressing the Academy in opposition to his
quondam friend Huet. Their friendship was first
interrupted by the publication of Origen's Commentaries, in which Bochart accused Huet of having intentionally omitted a passage on the Gospel
of St. Matthew, because it was against the doctrine
of transubstantiation, although Huet pretended
that the omission was accidental.

There has seldom been a Court where individual
character had so much play as in that of Christina.
No cold formality brought genius and mediocrity
to the same dull level. Sometimes the speculations
of philosophy prevailed, sometimes the fire of wit:

the gay young Queen was ever ready for intellectual exercise: she drew out every one, and made
her palace a stage on which the most opposite
characters figured: they followed in quick succession dazzling, delighting, or provoking; but ever
in the centre was the same bright, intelligent face;
the eyes which seemed to penetrate the thoughts
of every speaker before they found utterance; the
mind by which the subtlest arguments were understood as soon as stated, nay divined when only
half expressed.

Her patronage, indiscriminate as it may sometimes appear, was not without a purpose. She
rescued Sweden from a state of intellectual isola-
tion, and brought about a connection in science and
art between the North and the South of Europe.
She made an important link in the chain which
now unites the learned of all countries.

Bourdelot sometimes arranged comic scenes
without much regard for the annoyance they might
cause, the result of which was to draw down a bitter
hostility on his own head.

The performance of Naudé and Meibom was of
this nature. Naudé possessed both wit and learning: he was one of the Queen's librarians, and his

anecdotes of his own times, called "Naudeana," are well known : he was one who could either play or take a joke. Meibom was a man of less genial character, who had expended a good deal of learning on trivial subjects, and was consequently rather touchy about his dignity. On his arrival at Stockholm he presented the Queen with his work on ancient music.* Naudé had also written a learned work on the dances of the ancients.

The mischievous Bourdelot persuaded the Queen to make them illustrate their works by a performance before the Court. Meibom was to sing, and Naudé to dance, in the ancient style.

As the knowledge they possessed of these arts was purely theoretical, it may easily be imagined that the performance was exquisitely ludicrous : the whole Court was convulsed with laughter, and the unfortunate performers were thoroughly disconcerted.

Naudé withdrew in silence, but the more excitable musician was so enraged as to strike the author of the mischief in the Queen's presence. Such an outrage could not be overlooked, and he

* Meibomii Antiquæ Musicæ Auctores Septem. 4to. Amsterdam, 1652.

was expelled from Sweden, but it was felt that it was indècorous in the Queen to be a party to such buffoonery. The age and character of Bochart had not saved him from a somewhat similar joke, although in his case Christina was deceived by Bourdelot, who assured her that Bochart was a very fine flute player, but so shy that nothing less than a positive command would induce him to perform.

It must not, however, be supposed that Christina depreciated or ridiculed the fine arts, for everything calculated to refine the mind or the taste received its share of her consideration.

Adjoining her library was a picture gallery, containing fine specimens by the Carracci, Titian, Paul Veronese, and Correggio : she had many beautiful statues in marble and alabaster : her collection of medals was exceedingly valuable, and she was considered one of the best judges of her time. She sent Swedish artists to study the work of the great masters in Italy. If no great genius appeared in this line, it was not for want of encouragement, but because the spirit of the seventeenth century was more inclined to science than to art.

Bourdelot has been occasionally mentioned as a person who was generally believed to have exercised a very injurious influence on Christina, and it will now be desirable to examine more particularly his conduct at the Swedish Court.

He was a native of Sens, and his proper name was Michon. His father was a barber, who married a lady of good family named Bourdelot. The son, who will in future be called by his adopted name, was brought up as an apothecary in his native place, and was afterwards sent to Paris in the hope that he might receive some assistance from his mother's relations. His talent, or his good fortune, soon brought him into notice, and he became physician to the great Condé. Very little is recorded of his professional qualifications, but it appears that he was quick and clever, that he sang and painted, had a good deal of wit, and knew the useful art of making himself agreeable.

When Salmasius left Sweden, and left his enemy Vossius behind him, he was afraid that Christina might be induced to withdraw his pension; and to prevent this, he wished to leave some friend to protect his interests.

He made proposals to Ménage, but the Swedish

winter had great terrors for men of pleasure, and
Ménage preferred remaining in Paris. Salmasius
then addressed himself to Guy Patin, who was a
man of very similar character and attainments,
and whose jokes and anecdotes, called " Patineana,"
strongly resemble the " Menagiana," and are often
bound in the same volume.

Patin also feared the Northern climate, and
Salmasius then thought of Bourdelot, who was his
countryman, and who was willing to undertake
any adventure that was likely to result in his own
advantage.

Bourdelot came to Sweden early in 1652, where
the introduction of Salmasius, and his own reputation as physician to one of the French royal family,
soon attracted Christina's notice. The art of
medicine was in a very low state in Sweden. The
first professor had established himself there only
thirty years before, and he combined the practice
of medicine with that of astrology. A school of
anatomy was founded in 1637, but very little progress was made in the science, because the dissec-
tion of human subjects was forbidden.

From the time that Christina became Bourdelot's patient a marked improvement took place in

her health.   Her temperament was nervous and
irritable, and her constitution. was weakened by
overwork, and by injudicious diet.   She was constantly subject to debility, low fever, and fainting-
fits ; symptoms for which her doctors had hitherto
prescribed bleeding.   Bourdelot ordered warm
baths and change of diet, and he forbade all kinds
of study or excitement until her health improved.
Under his care the attacks soon began to abate,
and Christina always said that, next to God, she
had to thank Bourdelot for her life.   Her favour
naturally increased, and he well knew how to
make the most of it.   He thoroughly understood
the art of conversation, and the readiness with
which he used his knowledge made it seem much
greater than it really was.   He judged rightly that
his treatment would be incomplete unless he could
influence his patient's mind, and he strove to
set her against those pedants who overtaxed her
strength in studies with which he had little sympathy.   The medicine that he used for this purpose
was ridicule.   He had an endless store of jokes
about these savants, and he related them with a
degree of sarcastic humour which was irresistible.
The consequence was that Christina withdrew her-

self from the scholars and statesmen to converse with the physician.

The hatred which he thus raised against himself became universal. The nobles, who had blamed her devotion to learning, now denounced her neglect of it, and they were joined by the clergy, who complained of Bourdelot's irreligion. The last charge was not without foundation, for he did not refrain from exercising his wit on the most sacred subjects.

His enemies loudly proclaimed his ignorance, and the fate of some courtiers who consulted him professionally, seemed to warrant the accusation, for it was said that in a short time his patients were beyond the reach of medicine.

It is probable that ignorance was not his worst quality, for his abilities were esteemed by Naudé, Salmasius, and Gassendi. It was said that the Pope at one time contemplated making him a Cardinal, for which dignity he was at least as well fitted as Vossius was to be Canon of Windsor.

The clergy took the lead in the demonstration against the obnoxious favourite, and prepared a

* Chanut, Vol. III., p. 161.

remonstrance which dwelt on his unorthodox
opinions. It was not easy to get one of their
own body to present this document to Christina,
for they knew that the individual who put himself
forward in this matter, would have small chance
of ecclesiastical preferment.

At last Maria Leonora, who was a zealous
Lutheran, and had always stood well with the
clergy, offered to convey the remonstrance to her
daughter. It was not without some fear and
anxiety that the Queen Dowager approached the
subject; she spoke of the devotion of Gustavus
Adolphus to the true faith, and then turned the
conversation to the impiety of Bourdelot.

Christina thanked her for the hint, but said
that religious disputes were too deep for them, and
should rather be left to the priests. Maria Leonora, however, persisted in the subject, when at
last her daughter exclaimed: " I know well who
have induced your Majesty to take this step, but I
will make them repent of their interference."

She then quitted the room abruptly, leaving her
mother in tears.

Some hours afterwards she endeavoured to
soothe her, but without making any concession,

and the result of the dispute was that Maria Leonora left the Court and retired to Nyköping. Christina had never behaved amiably to her mother, and the consequences recoiled on herself; for although Maria Leonora's arguments may have been weak, her instincts were right, and Christina's extraordinary favour to Bourdelot was made an excuse for grave accusations by her enemies.

Magnus de la Gardie was a less disinterested adviser. He chafed at his own favour being obscured by a low-born foreigner.

He complained to the Queen in January, 1653, that her doctor prejudiced her against him, as well as against the rest of the Swedish nobility. During the conversation Bourdelot himself came in, and was informed directly by the Queen of the charge against him. He denied the accusation, and De la Gardie offered to produce two witnesses who could prove it, but when they were confronted with Bourdelot they denied all knowledge of the affair.

The quarrel was made up for the time, but the Count renewed his attack in May, when he presented a formal memorial to the Queen, which stated that he and several of the highest officers wished to leave the Court unless Bourdelot was dismissed. Christina was irritated at this dictation, but she knew that the hostility to Bourdelot was not altogether undeserved, and she wisely determined to let him go.

She obtained from the French Court the grant of an Abbey for her discarded favourite, but Bourdelot quarrelled so much with his monks, that he spent most of his time in Paris, where he lived neither respectably nor happily.

Christina told Chanut soon afterwards that she knew Bourdelot's faults, but could not forget his services, amongst which was that of saving her life.

Although she thus provided for her doctor, it was clear that she did not remember him with any particular tenderness, for she sometimes spoke of him with a degree of contempt which might have been caused by her appreciation of his moral character, but which was probably also occasioned by disgust at the annoyance she had suffered on his account.

About two months after his departure, a parcel arrived from Paris, in which Bourdelot enclosed a letter. The Queen took it up, but as soon as she recognized the writing, she said that it smelt of medicine, and threw it away unopened.

It is to be remarked that she never forsook those whom she esteemed, and never thought she had sufficiently repaid them; but she recompensed the services of those whom she did not esteem, and then considered that they had no further claims upon her; she used them in the employments for which they were fit, without always expecting a combination of good qualities in the same person. She knew that an able scholar, a brave soldier, a clever doctor, or a skilful diplomatist, might be neither modest, pious, honourable, nor sincere, but she thought it better to have books well edited, battles won, health restored, and treaties successfully concluded, rather than to employ the most amiable and exemplary men who were incapable. The summary way in which she dismissed her favourites, is a strong proof that they were never her lovers. Courageous as Christina was, she would never have dared to provoke them so far if she had been thus at their mercy.

None of these men ever hinted that he had been the favoured one, although each, when he was supplanted by a rival, did not scruple to assert that a guilty passion was the cause of her preference.

Magnus de la Gardie had received more substantial proofs of the Queen's bounty than any one else, but even he was dismissed when he assumed the right to criticize her behaviour to others. It was with some difficulty that he recovered a portion of her favour after the quarrel with Bourdelot.

His jealousy next showed itself against Steinberg, who had saved the Queen's life in the following manner :—

Christina went one morning at four o'clock to inspect some ships which were being equipped at Stockholm. In order to look closely at some part of a vessel, she stood on a plank which was suspended over the water. Admiral Fleming was by her side, when unfortunately his foot slipped, and as he was falling he involuntarily caught hold of the Queen's dress, and dragged her with him. Steinberg, who was the Groom in Waiting, jumped into the water, and with some difficulty supported the Queen until further assistance arrived.

Christina had fallen head-foremost into the water, and was half drowned, but she showed her presence of mind and generosity by giving orders about the Admiral before she was out of the water herself. The old man had sunk, but kept his hold of the Queen's dress with the desperate grasp of a drowning man. So far from blaming him for this, after they were both rescued, she congratulated him on having adopted the only course which could have saved his life. She dined in public afterwards, and spoke of the accident with the same coolness that she had shown at the time. She said that she was so used to drink cold water that an extra quantity would not hurt her, although she should certainly have preferred it fresh and clean; but she slily hinted that so large a draught of an unaccustomed beverage might disagree with the Admiral.

It was quite natural that Christina should show some favour to Steinberg after this adventure. He was the son of a general who had served in the Thirty Years' War, and it was not an unsuitable reward for the young man that he was ennobled, and received, as the device for his coat of arms, a lion rising from the waves.

Shortly after the departure of Bourdelot, Magnus was one day conversing with the Queen, when he took the opportunity to expatiate on his truth and devotion to her, and to hint that these good qualities had drawn enmity upon himself. "He had heard with grief how Her Majesty misunderstood him, and how she had said that he had committed an act of treachery which the Prince would one day repay." He added that all this was told him by a person who had it direct from Her Majesty. He refused for a long time to say who this person was, but at last named Steinberg.

"That is impossible!" said Christina; "Steinberg is too honourable a man to invent such falsehoods. I have so good an opinion of him, that if he asserted I had said this, 1 should believe it myself: I will investigate the matter at once!" Upon this she rang a bell, and ordered Steinberg and some Senators who were in an adjoining room to be summoned.

This was not what De la Gardie had intended; he endeavoured to stop the proceedings, and entreated the Queen to consider his communication as confidential. He could not prevent her from asking Steinberg whether she had ever used the expressions which were attributed to her. Steinberg declared positively that she had never done

so. The Count now began to prevaricate, and said
that he had not heard it from Steinberg himself,
but through a third person. Steinberg said that it
concerned his honour to know who this third person was, but De la Gardie obstinately refused to
give up the name.

In this manner the conversation ended for the
day, but Christina encouraged Steinberg to insist
on knowing the name of the person who had put
these words into his mouth, and she expressed her
wish to be freed from the Count's complaints and
ill-temper.

Steinberg called next day on the Count, who
received him with compliments and courtly phrases,
said that he was convinced of his honour, and laid
all the blame on the unknown reporter. Steinberg answered bluntly that he should believe the
falsehood was invented by the Count himself, unless he gave up the name of his informant. Even
this appeal failed, and it was only in consequence
of a peremptory order from the Queen that De la
Gardie named a Colonel Schlippenbach as the
author of the story.

This officer was not in Stockholm at the time,
but he was immediately sent for, not however be-

fóre he had been visited by four of the Count's
followers, who begged him to corroborate the statement made by their patron.   Schlippenbach refused to do this, and said that he would state the
truth to the Queen, and prove himself an honourable man.

On his arrival he was immediately confronted
with De la Gardie, when he said that he had never
heard any such story from Steinberg, and tha
he did not know what the Count meant.   He
added, that he had only once spoken to the Count
about Steinberg, and on that occasion De la Gardie
had expressed both jealousy and dislike for the
young man.

Christina hinted to De la Gardie that his proper
course would be to call out Schlippenbach, but he
did not think this suited his dignity.

He requested permission to retire into the
country, and very insolently added a demand that
Schlippenbach should be dismissed.

Christina answered that she not only permitted,
but ordered him to leave the Court until he could clear
his honour : she added that the request for Schlippenbach's dismissal was an unreasonable one, which
she could by no means grant.

De la Gardie was abject in disgrace as he had
been insolent in prosperity. He wrote to solicit
an interview with the Queen before he left the
Court, but she refused his prayer, and told him
severely that he had himself published a secret
that she had determined to conceal all her life,
viz., that he was unworthy of the favour she had
shown him.

De la Gardie condescended to beg the good
offices of his old opponent Oxenstiern.

The Chancellor gave a courteous and dignified
answer: he said that he had never interfered in
such matters, and that once, when invited by Gustavus Adolphus to do so, he had answered that he
would rather resign his office. He concluded by
saying that "age and ill-health rendered him
incapable of giving advice." Perhaps de la Gardie
remembered that in his prosperity he had used this
very expression to depreciate the old man's
opinion.*

Although Oxenstiern could not altogether
conceal his contempt, he was far too noble to revenge himself for former impertinences.

* Archenholtz. Vol. I., p. 369.

The Queen sent him a copy of her letter to the disgraced favourite, and said, " I send you my letter to Count Magnus, and wish either for your approval or your advice. I have always sought first to do what is right, and next to secure the approbation of every honest man." Oxenstiern thanked her for her confidence, and without entering into the merits of the case, reminded her of the great services of his old friend, Jacob de la Gardie, the father of Magnus.

In a private letter to his son Erik he spoke with less reserve, and said that Magnus knew how to bear neither prosperity nor adversity.

Notwithstanding the slight estimation in which Magnus was held, the aristocratic party did not lose an opportunity of embarrassing Christina: they framed a remonstrance, in which they said it was not constitutional to dismiss a high Officer of State in so summary a way. The fact was, however, that De la Gardie had tendered his own resignation.

The Prince Charles Gustavus interceded for his brother-in-law without success. Christina told him that the disgraced favourite deserved no consideration from him, since he had dissuaded her from the marriage which Charles Gustavus so much desired.* If this was true, it was probably " the act of treachery which the Prince would one day repay," but it would seem to indicate that Christina in some degree regretted the refusal she had given to Charles Gustavus.

It is certain that for the rest of their lives a bitter animosity existed between the Queen and De la Gardie. She expressed resentment against those who ventured even to visit him, and he took every opportunity to affront her from whom he had received such innumerable benefits, the moment that he could do so with safety. At her abdication, even those most opposed to her government were so struck with admiration or remorse, that they were unable to conceal their emotion. Magnus de le Gardie alone exulted openly at the political death of his benefactress,

---

* Chanut says, she told the Prince, 'que le Compte Magnus etoit indigne qu'il eut aucune affection pour lui, ni aucune compassion de sa disgrace : qu'elle vouloit qu'il sçeut, que si elle ne l'avoit pas épousé, il en etoit la cause. . . . .

'Elle ne doutoit point qu'elle n'eut consenty au mariage, mais que le Compte l'en avoit toujours detournée.'—Chanut, Vol. III., p. 315.

and when she afterwards visited Sweden, he took the lead in everything calculated to injure or annoy her.*

* 'Her old favourite, Magnus de la Gardie, spoke against her being allowed to enter the kingdom for fear of commotions among the peasants.'—F. F. Carlsson. 'Sveriges Historia under Konungarne ap Pfalziska Huset.' Kap. 6.

CHAPTER II.

Preparations for the Queen's Coronation—Her Public Entry
into Stockholm—Ceremonies and Fêtes on the Occasion—
Lavish Profusion of the Queen—Her Personal Appearance
—Her Intention to Abdicate, and the Motives that led to
this Decision—The Remonstrances of Oxenstiern and the
Council—Conduct of Charles Gustavus at this Juncture—
The Queen's Postponement of the Decisive Step—Her
Mediation between France and Spain—Dissuades Condé
from his Criminal Enterprise against France—Letter to the
Duke of Orleans—The Conspiracy of Messenius—Life and
Character of Messenius and his Family— Professional
Rivalry of John Messenius and Rudbeck—Imprisonment
and Death of the Former—Arnold Messenius, the Elder—
Treated with severity by Gustavus Adolphus, but favoured
by Christina—Persuades his son to join him in measures of
hostility against the Queen—Imaginary Dialogue between
Christina and her Master of the Ceremonies—Anonymous
Poem addressed to Charles Gustavus—Conduct of the
Queen on becoming acquainted with the Conspiracy—Ex-
amination and Trial of the two Messenii—Their Execution
—Cromwell proposes an Alliance between England and
Sweden—Dutch Hostility to the English Commonwealth—

SEVERAL of the favourites and literary men at Christina's Court have been mentioned without regard to the period at which they appeared, because they were so connected with one another, that it would be difficult to speak of each in his own place.

It is necessary to revert to some of the more important public events in Christina's life.

Her coronation had been deferred on account of the war, and of the internal troubles in Sweden, but preparations were made for celebrating it with unusual magnificence in 1650.

It was at first intended that the ceremony should take place at Upsala, for an old tradition existed in Sweden, that any sovereign who was crowned at Stockholm would have a short reign. The ancient capital, however, had very little accommodation, for it had not been enlarged and beautified like Stockholm. The crowd of generals, nobles, and officials, who claimed a place in the pageant, must have been encamped outside the walls. It was therefore determined to waive the superstitious scruples, and to crown the young Queen at Stockholm.

The festivities began even before the day of the coronation. On the 11th of October Christina went to stay with the Grand Marshal, Jacob de la Gardie. She was received with great magnificence: fountains of red and white wine played from mid-day until evening, and gave the populace the first taste of that extravagance for which

Christina was blamed by those who were its chief promoters.

It must, however, be confessed that she took no steps to check the general dissipation. The example was set by grave senators and nobles; successful warriors laid at her feet the trophies they had won; poets and philosophers added the intoxicating incense of their praise; ambassadors and princes all swelled the chorus. A young lady of twenty-four would indeed have been a philosopher if she had not been in some degree fascinated by the general homage she received.

On the 17th of October she entered Stockholm, and forty men-of-war, anchored under the castle, greeted her with a salute of 1,800 guns. She passed under three triumphal arches, on which were recorded the names of the victories gained by her generals. The captured banners waved over the arches, and not only added to the pomp, but gave an unmistakable evidence of her power. The procession lasted several hours, but the display did not end with the short Northern day. As soon as the darkness set in, fireworks were exhibited on such a scale that the whole city was covered with a canopy of smoke. It was an omen that clouds would soon obscure the splendour with which the young Queen dazzled all beholders. Her entry took place on Thursday, and the two following days were spent in completing the arrangements for the ceremony, and in settling matters of precedence.

If some compromises had not been arranged, Christina's coronation might have been deferred to another year. It was the etiquette for all members of the Council to take precedence of the generals, but the haughty chiefs, who had ruled whole provinces in Germany, refused to give place to civil officers, some of whom were obscure men. It was proposed to obviate the objection by letting the generals sit backwards in the carriages of the five dignitaries, but this also was objected to; and it was at last arranged that their carriages should not appear at all in the procession, but that the generals themselves should come on horseback, and should have a place near the Queen.

The coronation took place on Sunday; her old friend and tutor, Matthiæ, preached the sermon, and the Archbishop Lenæus placed the crown on her head. The Grand Marshal, Jacob de la Gardie, did not furnish the least interesting part of the spectacle. The veteran was now totally blind, but he would not, on that account, forfeit his right to bear the sword of state. He was led by his son, John Casimir, and no one could grudge him the honour who recollected how valiantly he had fought for Sweden. Magnus de la Gardie carried the royal banner, and the other dignitaries bore the gold key, the gold apple, the sceptre, and the crown.

The Lutheran Church at that time did not object to festivals on the Sabbath, and the fireworks were consequently repeated, and wine flowed in such profusion for the populace, that many of them were killed in drunken frays.

A few days afterwards, Charles Gustavus gave a fête, in which some novel shows were introduced. Vehicles, covered with people in glittering attire, seemed to move along of their own accord; and a hill, which represented Mount Parnassus, with muses and goddesses upon it, progressed in the same way.

Charles Gustavus also gave a ball in honour of the Queen's birthday, which she appreciated so much, as to dance at it until seven in the morning.

The rest of the nobility followed the example in giving festivals and balls, and a custom was introduced of presenting a nosegay after the last dance, to the one among the guests who they proposed should entertain them the next evening. He was always expected to accept the challenge, and so the round of dissipation continued.

In the midst of these festivities, winter set in with such severity that many persons died of cold, among whom were Torstenson's wife, and the once beautiful Ebba Brahe.

The excessive gaiety which accompanied and followed the coronation, was productive of many evils. Magnificence degenerated into extravagance and prodigality, both with the Court in general, and with the Queen herself. She lavished estates, pensions, and gold chains on all sides, and even larger revenues would have been injured by such profuseness.

Christina had now reached the height of her glory. Her fame had spread beyond the regions of the North, and all Europe viewed her with admiration and curiosity. Panegyrics were addressed to her from all parts, and medals were struck in honour of her. Foreign Courts, and especially that of France, were eager to obtain portraits of the famous Northern queen.

Christina was rather below the average height, but both her manner and her appearance were majestic. Her eyes were blue, very large and well opened, her nose was aquiline, her mouth large but well-formed, and her teeth beautiful. Her voice was generally soft, but when angry, it was loud, and resembled that of a man. The expression of her countenance continually varied; it was generally very animated, but at times it was pensive, though serene. She thought so little of her appearance, that her toilet seldom occupied her more than a quarter of an hour. Her hair, which was very fine, flowed in a negligent profusion that was not unbecoming to her.

Her attendants partook of her carelessness, for they often allowed her to appear with sleeves either torn or soiled with ink. When remonstrated with for the neglect of her personal appearance, she answered, that such cares were only suited to idle people.

All those who had rendered any service to the State, had been waiting for their reward until her accession, and the Regents had often relieved themselves from embarrassment by postponing any substantial acknowledgment to this time. The finances were in such a condition that it would have been difficult to recompense even those who had the strongest claims. The strictest economy was required, but unfortunately Christina could not moderate her love of giving : she made some retrenchments in her household, but these were not sufficient to supply her liberality to everyone who approached her.

She appeared, after her coronation, to have abandoned all attempts to check the nobles.

The succession of fêtes had brought her into more intimate connection with them, and from that time she relaxed in her efforts to protect the other orders.

Her promises to redress the grievances of the commoners had not been redeemed, and the thought must sometimes have forced itself upon her, how she should meet them at the next Diet. The impossibility of doing justice to the people without offending the nobles, and the difficulty of avoiding bankruptcy without resuming the Crown lands, were two urgent causes of her abdication. The personal honour of her successor would not be pledged to the alienation of the Crown domains, and he might repudiate the acts by which she was fatally bound.*

Her intention to abdicate became known soon after her coronation, but she had entertained the idea long before.

Chanut says, in a letter, dated February, 1654, that she had apprised him of her intention six years before,† and in her answer to him, she says, that it was at least five years since she had communicated her resolution to him, but that she had thought of it herself for eight years.‡

Among the motives to this decision, was undoubtedly the desire of leisure.

---

* 'A manuscript exists in the Library at Upsala, in the writing of Christina and Charles Gustavus, which states the necessity for retrenchment. It also states that he would not be bound to alienate from the Crown all that had been promised by her.' F. F. Carlsson, 'Sveriges Historia under Konungarne af Pfalziska Huset.' Kap 5.

† Memoires de ce qui s'est passé en Suede: Tirez des depesches de M. Chanut. Tome III. P. 302. Paris, 1675.

‡ 'Je vous ai rendu compte autrefois des raisons qui m'ont obligées de persévérer dans le dessein de mon abdication Vous scavez que cette fantasie m'a duré long temps, et que que ce n'est qu 'apres y avoir pensé huit ans, que je me suis resolue de l'executer : il y a pour le moins cinq ans que je vous ay communiqué cette resolution.' Chanut. Tome. III. P. 306.

Her love of literature had become a passion; she was impressed with the idea that other occupations prevented her enjoyment of it, and she forgot how much of the homage she received was rendered to the Queen.

Her learning had never been directed to a particular subject, but was spread over the whole field of knowledge, and therefore, with all her talent, she was not likely to produce any great work herself. No place could be so favourable as the throne for exercising her peculiar aptness of balancing and appreciating all kinds of merit.

Her foreign favourites soon discovered that the most pleasing topics were the delicious climate and charming scenery of the South, together with the treasures of art and knowledge contained in those favoured regions.

Her constitution, both of mind and body, rendered her peculiarly liable to these impressions, and a very slight consideration of Scandinavian history is sufficient to show how active a motive the enjoyment of a finer climate may become even to rude and hardy men, who are accustomed to the rigours of a northern winter. Christina began to think the cold of Sweden insufferable, and its state of society slightly removed from barbarism; and her mother, who had little influence on her for good, was able to increase this vague feeling of discontent. In 1651 she began to show more favour to Oxenstiern and his party, as if to deprecate their opposition to her plans; and some Swedes, who were travelling in Italy, heard reports there of her approaching abdication and conversion.

Channt appears to have been the first person that was apprized of her intention: he dissuaded her earnestly from it without success, and renewed his efforts by the direction of his own court.

It soon ceased to be a secret; she informed Charles Gustavus of it during a journey to Nyköping. The prince had adopted an extremely cautious line of conduct. He took no part in public affairs, and resided chiefly in the country, where he occupied himself in field sports, and in improving his estate in Oland. He thought that Christina's communication was an artifice to test his loyalty, and accordingly he affected to dissuade her from an intention which he did not believe was sincere. Soon afterwards Oxenstiern and De la Gardie were told, and they also endeavoured to dissuade her from so extraordinary a resolution.

Rumours of her intended abdication soon reached the people, and they complained that the great expense of the coronation ought not to have been incurred. "Was it meant," they said, "only as a spectacle to amuse Her Majesty?"

The nobles were greatly alarmed, for they feared that her successor might reverse the decrees which granted them the Crown lands. They now regretted the vexatious opposition they had offered to the young Queen, and made every exertion to prevent her abdication.

The first public announcement of her intention was made in a speech to the Council on the 7th of August, 1651. She told them that she had considered the matter for five or six years; she did not therefore ask their opinion, but only their assistance to enable Charles Gustavus to succeed her without trouble or disturbance.

Oxenstiern replied that the matter was of the greatest importance, and must be accounted for to the whole Swedish nation; it therefore required deep and mature consideration.

Christina answered that the Prince's good qualities were well known, that he was already recognized as the Heir-Apparent, and there was therefore nothing which required consideration.

Having said this she left the room, and the Council held a long sitting, in which they determined unanimously to oppose her resolution.*

Their strongest reasons against her abdication were too delicate to mention, the fear of Christina's inconstancy, and of losing their newly acquired estates; but the Council dwelt at length on minor objections.

They said they could not obey Her Majesty's order to give their immediate consent, for her welfare, their own, and that of the country, were so deeply concerned, that they must pause, not only before they put her proposition into execution, but even before they allowed it to be made public.

"Even an elected king," they said, "is pledged to his subjects' protection, much more so an hereditary king. Your Majesty was born heir to the throne, your title was confirmed by the oaths we took on our knees, and these oaths were repeated at your coronation. Your Majesty also swore to be our Queen, and to rule us according

* Riksark. Rådsprot, d. 7 Aug., 1651. Apud Fryxell, p. 117.

to law. So solemn an engagement cannot be broken without each party being open to blame.

"God in His secret council knows, but we cannot venture to predict, what would be the result of your Majesty's abdication. We esteem the Prince for his many good qualities, but your Majesty is our Queen; you have knowledge, experience, and authority; you have ruled us with good fortune at home and abroad. It is the wisest course to be content, and not to seek changes, which seldom do good, and often do harm.

"We do not know that your Majesty would lead a more peaceful life after abdicating, for we are ignorant of the future; neither do we know that repose would be consistent with your Majesty's duty. All mankind are born to care and trouble, especially kings and rulers, whose duty it is to seek their pleasure and happiness in work.

"Your Majesty may sometimes be wearied with the multitude of affairs, and vexed at the complaints and opposition of your subjects, but this heavy load may be lightened by the assistance of the Prince, and of your Council."*

* Engestrom, 'Acta om Drottning Kristina.' Tome II.

This communication was signed by thirteen of the Council; it is evidently in the Chancellor's style, and was in his hand-writing.

On the 25th of October the Queen summoned them again, and a discussion ensued which lasted five hours and a half. The members tried every argument to shake her resolution, but in vain; the most they could obtain was the promise that no further steps should be taken before the meeting of the Diet.

Remonstrances now poured in, amongst which those from Chanut and from Salvius had the most effect. Charles Gustavus declared that he would never accept the crown, so long as Christina was alive and in health, and he begged the States to join their entreaties to his own, in order to avert so great a misfortune as her abdication.

The Council determined to make another appeal. Oxenstiern again prepared a memorial, which De la Gardie and Rosenhane were deputed to present. They undertook the duty reluctantly, and even on the way Rosenhane stopped several times, and wished to turn back, so great was his dread of encountering the Queen's wrath. De la Gardie had more confidence in his own favour with her, and forced Rosenhane to proceed.

As soon as they entered her presence she guessed their errand, and, rolling her large eyes upon them, asked what they wanted. De la Gardie said that they craved a private audience. This was granted, and the Queen, accompanied by Herman Fleming, led them into another apartment. When they read Oxenstiern's memorial, she was moved to tears, and appeared to waver in her resolution. But Fleming, who was in favour of the abdication, did more to defeat his object by an ill-timed observation, than the entreaties of the others were able to effect.

He praised her resolution, but said that if her abdication were deferred, circumstances might arise to render it impossible.

This speech had a directly contrary effect to what he intended. Christina took fire and said, "What! do you think my will is to be controlled? I will show you that it is not only free at present, but that it shall remain so."

She then dismissed the deputation with a more favourable answer than they expected.*

Soon after this the whole Council, accompanied by some deputies of the States, waited on the

* Rådsprot, den 21 Juli. M. G. De la Gardie's Berrättelse.

Queen. Oxenstiern was their spokesman. He thanked her in the name of the whole kingdom for the care she had taken of the public prosperity and peace, owing to which Sweden was now in a more flourishing condition than any of the neighbouring countries. He said that the Prince would not accept the government while she lived, everything would be therefore in confusion if she abdicated, and the consideration of such an unhappy state of things would alone be sufficient to disturb her expected tranquillity. He said that all those present with him were of the same opinion, and if she abdicated they would all resign their offices and employments, lest they should be made accountable to posterity for an event so injurious to the country. He added, in his usual sententious style, that glory consisted more in preservation than in acquisition, and that it would have been better if her administration had been less happy, than that it should be abandoned at a time when no one could contemplate it without admiration. His arguments were much the same as those the poet puts into the mouth of Ulysses, when he says :—

> " Perseverance, dear my Lord,
> Keeps honour bright : To have done, is to hang,
> Quite out of fashion, like a rusty nail,
> In monumental mockery."

Oxenstiern finished his address in a more im-
passioned tone than was usual to him. "Most
gracious Queen," said he, turning to Christina,
"are you dissatisfied with us?   Have we not
shown you sufficient reverence and obedience?
Deign to tell us plainly!   We will submit to
whatever your Majesty desires : we will endeavour
to please you better in future, for we are ready to
sacrifice both goods and life to maintain your
greatness, your dignity, and your rights. We know
that the Crown has great burdens, but we promise
to discharge them all, and to furnish you with
means so ample as may enable you to hold a more
brilliant Court than any Sovereign in the North
has ever done before."

The old man spoke with such earnestness and
emotion as to touch all who heard him.   Christina
was moved herself, and she consented to withdraw
her resignation on condition that she should not
be again solicited to marry.

She told some of her more intimate friends,
however, that her resolution was only postponed,
and not altered.

In the midst of affairs so interesting to herself
Christina was not a passive spectator of what

passed in the rest of Europe.   Faithful to the love
of peace she had already so conspicuously displayed,
she endeavoured to mediate between France and
Spain.   These countries continued to carry on a
war which had no definite object, and according to
the system of politics then in vogue, the ruler of a
rival state would have been justified in fomenting
their quarrels.   Christina was too enlightened to
believe that their hostility would benefit Sweden.
The letters which she wrote to the King of France
and the King of Spain, in 1651, were full of wisdom
and dignity, and she earnestly entreated them to
stop the useless effusion of blood.

The troubles of the Fronde did not tempt her
from this charitable and Christian course : she
wrote to her favourite hero, Condé, and urged him
to relinquish his criminal enterprises against his
own country, and she sent the following noble
letter to the Duke of Orleans :—

" Royal personages should not only call themselves brothers and cousins, but they should give
proofs of fraternal feelings when occasions offer.
The French arms have been too serviceable in the
establishment of my power and glory, for me to
view with indifference those Frenchmen, whom no

one else could conquer, destroying one another.

" Your Royal Highness has too much experience
to be ignorant that God sends no heavier scourge
to a nation than civil war: such a war is generally
more cruel and more bitter than any other, although it is often kindled on paltry excuses, and
for insignificant causes. The ruin is incomparably
greater than that caused by other wars; for although both the contending parties assert that
they take up arms to save the State, they both
assist to lacerate it, and a good King regrets even
victories which are won over his own subjects."

She also wrote to the Parliament of Paris, and
offered her mediation with the Court. They took
her advice in good part, but the Court resented
her interference, and when Christina found that
no good was to be done, she adroitly threw the
blame on her agent for having given her letter to
the Parliament without having first obtained the
sanction of the Ministry.

Sweden did not pass quite scathless through this
period of general disturbance. The conspiracy of
Messenius showed that the elements of disorder
were smouldering in the North, although they did
not blaze out as in England, France, and Naples.

The history and character of Messenius and his family are too strange to be passed over without notice.

The grandfather of the conspirator was John Messenius, who was born at Wadstena in 1579. The undecided state of religious opinion in Sweden under John III. has been already mentioned, and had a particular influence on the career of Messenius. He was educated at the Jesuits' College, at Braunsberg, where he went through the usual course of study with great credit, and became a Doctor of Philosophy.

To great natural abilities, Messenius united profound historical and theological learning, great eloquence, and extraordinary industry.

These qualities were counterbalanced by a bad disposition, a bitterness and selfishness which were made more apparent by a vehement temper.

He remained for some time in the service of the Polish Vasas, but his success in the Catholic country did not correspond with his abilities, and still less with his pretensions.

In 1608, he returned to Sweden, but that country had become strictly Lutheran under Charles IX., and Messenius, therefore, professed himself a Protestant, although it is probable that in reality he retained his own faith, and only pretended a conversion without which he could have had no hope of advancement, and little chance even of safety in Sweden. Whether sincere or not, he took an oath of fealty to Charles IX., and published some abusive writings against his old friends the Jesuits.

He flattered the King by a genealogy, in which he gravely traced the royal pedigree from Antenor of Troy.

His zeal and heraldic lore did not remain unrewarded, for he was appointed a Professor of the University of Upsala.

His career at first was brilliant. The students flocked to his classes, which were managed with unusual industry and ability.

It was said that he did more work than all the other professors put together.

He did not pay the same attention to the good conduct of his pupils, as to their instruction; the behaviour of the young nobility at the University was often very disorderly, and Messenius, whose great object was popularity, connived at a very lax state of discipline. Some of the youths, who had committed serious outrages, were cited before the Consistory, but Messenius openly maintained that they were not under its authority, and were only responsible to him for their conduct.

He was in his turn summoned before the Chapter, when he sent an insulting answer, that they and their Archbishop might go to the devil.

The most remarkable of his contemporaries at Upsala, was John Rudbeck. A violent feud raged between the two professors, which extended to their pupils. Fierce battles took place in the streets between the hostile parties, whose conduct resembled the turbulence of mediæval barons and their retainers, rather than the emulation of rival scholars.

Such a state of things could not be tolerated, and the Chapter prohibited both Messenius and Rudbeck from having any private pupils. Rudbeck submitted, but Messenius repeated his insolent defiance, and the authority of the Chapter was so undefined, or so difficult to put in execution, that even yet no steps were taken to punish his outrageous conduct.

About this time, the Rector of the University died, and Rudbeck was chosen to fill his place.

The pride and resentment of Messenius were in-
flamed almost to madness at his rival's success.
He was present with his pupils at the new Rector's
opening address, and interrupted him with coarse
abuse.   As a climax to his violence, he armed himself with a sword and target, and attacked Rudbeck.

Accounts of the wild proceedings at Upsala soon
reached Gustavus Adolphus, who sent Oxerstiern
and some bishops to investigate the whole affair.

The inquiry was pursued with a spirit of moderation, for it was felt that the two chief culprits
were men whose talents were an honour to Sweden.
They could not be allowed to remain in their posts
at Upsala, but Rudbeck was made Bishop of
Westerås, and Messenius was appointed Keeper of
the Archives at Stockholm.

Messenius, however, could hardly breathe except in an atmosphere of strife.   He not only
quarrelled with everyone about him, but he was
accused of carrying on a traitorous correspondence
with the Polish Vasas, in which he urged them to
attack Sweden.   It does not appear that the
proofs of this treason are now in existence, but its
probability has been shown by a letter from Mes-

senius, in which he owned his undiminished attachment to the Roman Church, and said that he only conformed to the Lutheran rites outwardly and by compulsion. His judges, among whom was Oxenstiern, considered that his guilt was proved, and they sentenced him to death, but Gustavus Adolphus commuted the punishment to imprisonment for life.

The unfortunate man was sent to Kajaneborg in Finland. He sailed from Stockholm to Wasa, and from thence was carried by land to the verge of the Arctic circle, in the depth of winter. The fortress was built between Uleå and the Russian frontier, partly upon an island, and partly upon piles, so that the river flowed beneath it. A waterfall above, and another below, kept the place enveloped in a cold spray, which rapid motion alone prevented from becoming ice. Nothing but a footpath led to this wretched spot: the country around was almost desert, and the few inhabitants were Fins, who did not understand a word of Swedish. Such was the prison of the learned Messenius, and his misery was increased by the unwonted harshness of the King, who gave orders that the prisoner should be treated with the greatest strictness.

Even the sufferings he underwent did not subdue his fiery temper; a good deal of his energy was spent in provoking his keepers, who repaid him with harsh and brutal treatment.

His incarceration lasted nineteen years, but a great part of this dreary time was spent in a manner worthy of his eminent talents.

He was allowed the consolation of books, and during his captivity he wrote the History of Sweden, the first work which deserved the name of a history in that language.

After the death of Gustavus Adolphus, his treatment was improved. He was removed to the more habitable town of Uleå, and the Regents sent a person to examine and report on the merit of his work.

He might probably have regained his liberty, but with his usual perversity he thought that the Regents wished to appropriate the fame and honour of his book.

While disputing about the terms on which he would give Sweden the benefit of his labours, he was at last set free by the hand of death.

His son, Arnold John Messenius, had been with him at Kajaneborg, but was taken away, that he might not be brought up as a Roman Catholic. A still more cruel proceeding was using the evidence of the boy against his father, in reference to some intrigues with the Popish rulers in Poland.

Arnold Messenius managed to escape from Sweden, but when he heard that his father was treated with increased rigour on that account, he returned voluntarily, and surrendered himself into the hands of his enemies. Neither his youth nor his filial piety moved his stern judge. Even his innocence did not avail him; for Gustavus Adolphus ordered him to be imprisoned, although no evidence was found against him.

Arnold Messenius was confined two years in Stockholm, and fourteen years in Finland. At the end of that time Brahe was Governor-General of Finland. He procured the release of Messenius with considerable difficulty, after much opposition from Oxenstiern, who said that Messenius was a dangerous character, and would make mischief among the people.

Oxenstiern formed a more correct estimate of his character than either Brahe or Christina, yet their treatment was both more generous and more just. If she had had a person of a better disposition than Messenius to deal with, Christina's behaviour would even have been politic. She endeavoured to atone for the harshness and injustice with which he had been treated. She engaged him to continue his father's book; she gave him an estate and ennobled him; and when the nobles objected to receive him in their chamber, she sent them a peremptory order to admit him.

Messenius was neither softened by adversity nor improved by prosperity. He was harsh to his inferiors, insolent to his equals, and ungrateful to his benefactress. The peasants on his estate complained of his injustice and cruelty, and he was on bad terms with all his neighbours. He resisted some just claims of his own sister's, and the cause was referred to law. In accordance with a judgment given against him, Christina obliged him to make restitution to his sister. From that time he became an agitator against the government.

The generosity of Christina was as ineffectual as the severity of her father, and Messenius not only excited the Swedish peasants to revolt, but entered into correspondence with the Polish Pretender.

His son, also named Arnold Messenius, was born in 1629, and at the age of sixteen was made a page in the household of Charles Gustavus. In 1651 the young man paid a visit to his father, and readily joined in his hostility to the Queen. They were more bitter than ever when Christina retracted her resignation, and their wrath was also extended to those advisers who had persuaded her to remain on the throne. The elder Messenius invented the most absurd and contradictory accusations against the Queen and her Ministers, which were exaggerated by the heated imagination of his son. He wrote an anonymous poem to his patron, Charles Gustavus, the wickedness of which was equalled by its folly. He said that Christina was bringing everything to ruin, and that she cared for nothing but sport and pleasure.

He introduced an imaginary dialogue between the Queen and her master of the ceremonies.

" Beaulieu," she says, " how much does a ballet cost? "

" About 10,000 dollars, your Majesty."

" What! " says the Queen, " is that all? Get the money directly from the Treasurer."

She then turns to her Chamberlain, John Holm, " what do people talk about in the town?"

" They find the time heavy and tedious since

your Majesty no longer dances," is the courtier's reply.

" Well, Beaulieu," says the Queen, " prepare a ball, for we must amuse the people. How much will it cost? "

" About 20,000 dollars, your Majesty."

" Good," she replies, " go to the Treasurer and get the money."

The poem after this, rather inconsistently, represents the Queen as the victim of Oxenstiern and De la Gardie.

They alienated the Crown lands to reduce the royal authority. They gave freedom of trade to Stockholm, to bribe the people against the Crown. They engaged John Matthiæ to educate the Queen in a manner to render her unfit for government. They sent Charles Gustavus to the German war, and placed him, like another Uriah, in the thickest of the fight, that they might get rid of him.

His proposed marriage with the Queen was broken off through the intrigues of Matthiæ and Ebba Brahe, and this noble lady had everything prepared to poison him if he could have been inveigled to Jacobsdal. The Prince is then earnestly recommended to forestall his enemies, and to inaugurate a popular government by a blood bath even more atrocious than that of Christian the Tyrant. He is advised to collect troops at Stockholm on various pretences; to kill Christina, with all the nobles, and then to resume the crown lands, and reign in peace.

The Prince showed the letter to his confidant, Colonel Wurtz, who immediately suspected the elder Messenius to be the author, on account of expressions he had already heard from him.

Before Charles Gustavus took any further steps, Colonel Wurtz mentioned the letter to Messenius, so that if he were guilty he might have time to escape. In the meantime, the communication had been betrayed to Herman Fleming and the Queen —but it is remarkable that the first idea of every-one seems to have been to keep the matter secret. Fleming did not ask for an audience until Christina heard of the conspiracy from another quarter. He then made rather light of it, and pronounced it to be the work of some silly, hot-headed person. The Queen looked at him for some time in silence, and then replied, " What you say may be very true, my lord, but perhaps I know more about it than you do. I know, for instance, that the plot has been communicated to the Prince, and I should like to see what he will do. You are in his confidence—what do you think of it?"

Fleming answered that the Prince was too wise and too honourable to be concerned in such a plot, and that he would undoubtedly send notice of it to Her Majesty.

Christina, in her fearless way, said that she was inclined to remain quiet until the conspiracy broke out, that she might know with certainty who was guilty. Fleming, with difficulty, dissuaded her from this course, on the ground that it might cause unnecessary bloodshed.

The Prince's communication soon arrived; but it was calculated that exactly time enough had elapsed from the day of Fleming's interview for a messenger to go and return in all haste from Öland. It is, therefore, quite possible that Charles Gustavus only determined to tell Christina of the conspiracy when he found that she knew it already. It is most probable that he thought no serious plot was intended, and that he was unwilling to betray a e rson who evinced strong attachment to himself. He now hesitated no longer, but sent the letter to the Queen, under cover to Magnus de la Gardie.

It was accompanied by one from himself, in which he expressed his horror and indignation at the proposal made to him, and assured Her Majesty of his fidelity and devotion.

Christina at once suspected Messenius to be the author of the conspiracy. She produced the letter in the Council, and one of the members recognized the writing of his own secretary. This person was examined, and confessed that he had copied it at the request of young Messenius. The Queen herself examined the latter. At first he boldly denied the treason imputed to him; but presently he lost courage, burst into tears, and, falling at the Queen's feet, begged for mercy. He confessed that the statements contained in his letter were grounded on his father's conversation, but said that his father was not aware of its composition.

The elder Messenius was next examined. In his statements he only endeavoured to shield himself. "He believed the letter to be written by his son, but, if so, it was without his knowledge, and he abhorred the treason as much as anyone could do: he had served his country honourably, and had never used any treasonable expressions before his son, but had, on the contrary, warned him against seditious writings."

Young Messenius was less pusillanimous ; he appeared to glory in his performance, which he persisted in saying was inspired by his father, and by a leader of the popular party named Christopher of Fors.

As the examination proceeded, the elder Messenius contradicted all that he had said before, and confessed that he had frequently held treasonable conversations with his son, and with many others, among whom he named Bengt Skytte, Nils Nilsson, Christopher of Fors, Terserus, and Skunk.

His confession was mingled with sighs and tears, and he noticed, in a sentimental way, the divine justice which had caused him to be convicted on his son's testimony in the very room where he himself had given evidence against his father.

He bequeathed his library to the Queen, and begged for an easy death. He also asked permission to kiss her hand, which she granted.

He appeared not only willing, but anxious to give evidence against his accomplices : he gave full particulars of their treasonable expressions, and did his best to get them included in his own doom. He said that the most violent schemes proposed in the letter were the suggestion of Christopher of Fors.

No evidence, however, was adduced to support the accusation, and Christopher stoutly denied all knowledge of the treason.

Nils Nilsson was the next accused, and his examination caused some anxiety, for he had great influence with the people, and the charges against him seemed probable, because he had been a leader of the discontented peasants at the Diet of 1650.

Messenius swore that this man had proposed plans for general disturbances and changes of government, and that, when he saw the letter to Charles Gustavus, he said he hoped the Prince would take courage.

Nils Nilsson denied all this, and resisted the efforts of his accuser to make him out "just such another patriot as he was himself."

The trial, which was carried on under Christina's immediate superintendence, was remarkable for two things.

Although the torture was commonly practised, it was not resorted to on this occasion, and no one was found guilty without conclusive evidence. When it is remembered how generally the laws relating to treason were wrested to the destruction of any person obnoxious to the Government, it must be admitted that the Queen displayed singular fairness and moderation, and that her conduct was equally removed from violence and from weakness.

The two Messenii were executed, but no one else was punished.*

Christina had at first been much concerned at the fate of Charles I., but her ministers were in favour of the Parliament, and she had too much sense to let her personal feelings interfere with her policy. Charles had not deserved much favour from her, for at the time that he professed great friendship, he had secretly promised to assist Uladislaus of Poland in the invasion of Sweden.†

In March, 1650, the English Parliament sent two envoys with a complimentary letter to the Queen. She received them graciously, and seized

* Fryxell, Nionde Delen.
† Grauert, 'Kristina Königinn und ihr Hof.'

the opportunity of trying to introduce friendly relations between England and France.*

One of Cromwell's favourite projects was an intimate alliance between England and Sweden, by which means he thought the two great Protestant countries would be secured from any attack by the Catholic Powers.

This desire was increased by the impolitic conduct of the Dutch, who rejected his proffered friendship, and insulted St. John when he was sent to the Hague to propose a coalition between the two republics.

The States condoled with Charles II. on the execution of his father, and saluted him as king, and their policy was the more resented by the English Parliament, because none of the sovereigns of Europe ventured to pay the fugitive monarch a similar compliment, except the Czar of Russia, who broke off all intercourse with the revolutionary government, and expelled all English merchants from his dominions.†

The Dutch clergy were as devoted as the English to Charles I.; they compared his execu-

* Chanut, p. 371.
† Guizot's 'Life of Cromwell,' p. 208.

tion. to the martyrdom of St. Stephen,* and the very populace joined in demonstrations for the royal authority and against their own freedom.

Dorislaus, who was sent from England to Holland, in 1649, to propose a league of amity between the two republics, was murdered by some royalists the very day of his arrival at the Hague, and the assassins were allowed to depart unmolested.

The Stadholder, William II., who was married to a daughter of Charles I., was on the point of concluding a treaty with France, to carry on a war against the English Commonwealth, until the family of Stuart should be restored to the throne.

William's death, in 1650, did not diminish the hostility of the Orange faction, who were still desirous of involving their country in a war with England, in the hope of accomplishing the restoration of Charles II.

It is an instructive fact that when the Prince was restored to the throne, he not only forgot all his obligations to the Dutch, who had acted for his sake against their own interests, and in contradiction to their usual maxims of justice and

* Davis, 'History of Holland,' Vol. II., p. 675.

moderation, but he was base enough to assist his master, Louis XIV., in his unjust attack on the Netherlands. This was the only reward the Dutch reaped from the war in which the finest navies in the world tore one another to pieces, when Monk and Blake fought against De Ruyter and Van Tromp, and those kindred races which had hitherto shed their blood side by side in the defence of liberty, were provoked to fight one another with deadly animosity for the sake of an unworthy family.

One illustrious Dutchman reconciled the two nations, and revenged their wrongs on France and on the Stuarts. He hurled Charles's brother from the throne of his ancestors, and prepared for Louis XIV. an old age of vexation and disgrace.

Both Charles and Louis had made flattering proposals to the Prince of Orange himself. They offered to make him Sovereign of the provinces, under the protection of England and France, and they represented that Holland would be utterly ruined unless he agreed to the terms proposed. Neither of the profligate monarchs was capable of understanding William's noble character, when he answered, "I have thought of a means to avoid

beholding the ruin of my country, to die in the last ditch."

The ambassadors of the English Commonwealth were mobbed and insulted in Holland.

They resented this treatment deeply, and St. John employed himself actively, on his return to England, in carrying through Parliament the celebrated Navigation Act. The object of this Act was to injure the Dutch commerce, and especially their carrying trade. It decreed that no production of Asia, Africa, or America should be brought to England except in English vessels, manned by English crews, and that no production of Europe should be brought to England except in vessels belonging to that country of which it was the growth or manufacture.

These proofs of ill-will on each side, gave but too sure indications of the approaching war between the two republics, and Christina was the more inclined to receive the advances of Cromwell, because she had herself some reason to be dissatisfied with the Dutch.

The Swedish commerce had extended considerably under her administration, and Holland no longer monopolized the trade of the Baltic.

Sweden had an advantage possessed by no other state in her freedom from the Sound dues. The Dutch were galled at this immunity of their rivals, and endeavoured to make up for it by vexatious imposts on such Swedish vessels as came within their jurisdiction.

Trade, which ought to be a bond of union between nations, had hitherto been the most fruitful source of discord, for it was an established axiom that the prosperity of any nation was an injury to its neighbours.

About the time that war broke out between England and Holland, Cromwell determined on sending an ambassador to Sweden.

He chose Sir Bulstrode Whitelocke for the purpose, a man of considerable ability, one of whose recommendations was that he was inclined to be troublesome at home. The formal Puritan kept a regular journal of his residence at the young Queen's court, which is not only very amusing, but which is especially valuable, because Whitelocke was not a partial witness, and was by no means indulgent to dissipation and revelling. He was moreover so fond of gossip that he would not have failed to repeat any scandal at the Swedish Court.

In the whole of his journal, which fills two quarto volumes, there is not the slightest imputatation on Christina's character, and he found her entertainments so "genteel" that he seems to have partaken of them with considerable satisfaction. His greatest accusation against her was that she used to take the air in her coach on Sundays.*

The Dutch took alarm at Whitelocke's arrival in Sweden, and directed their envoy, Van Beunigen, to oppose the influence of the English minister in every possible way.

Van Beunigen, although a learned man, had not those common accomplishments which are indispensable at a court, and he never gained the same favour with Christina as she accorded to the other foreign ministers; and on his part he cherished and paraded unfriendly feelings towards the country in which he was residing.

It was said that wounded vanity had much to do with this. Christina once invited him to a hunting party, and gave orders that he should be provided with one of her best horses.

Her commands were too well obeyed. The

* Whitelocke's Swedish Embassy. 2nd Apl. 1654.

steed provided for the minister was a very lively one, and the groom, who shared in the popular prejudice against Dutchmen's riding, recommended Van Beunigen to choose a steadier animal, and good-naturedly urged him to exchange with one of the servants.

The scholar thought his honour was concerned, and positively refused to ride any other horse. He informed the groom that he was not a novice in the equestrian art; far from it, he had read every treatise on the subject from Xenophon d own-wards; he felt sure that no horse could resist so much knowledge.

Unfortunately the event did not turn out as he expected. Christina's steed made an absurd exhibition of his rider, and finally threw him; and though Van Beunigen had no one but himself to blame, he extended his resentment not only to the horses, but also to the government of Sweden.*

The English interpretations of Public Law were not very consistent at this time. The *Mare Clausum*, written by Selden, in 1635, was an attempt to justify, by argument, those rights of Great Britain over the surrounding seas, which

* Archenholtz. Tome I., p. 738.

had long been established by custom. These claims had been so strictly enforced, that when Henry IV. of France sent Sully to congratulate James I. on his accession, an English admiral fired on the envoy for presuming to hoist the French flag in the presence of an English squadron, and in sight of Calais.*

Although the English pretensions were not at all diminished in the time of Cromwell, yet one of Whitelocke's chief objects was to insist on the free navigation of the Sound, and to concert measures with Christina for enforcing this demand on Denmark. At the same time Swedish vessels trading with Holland, were captured by the English cruisers, and that right of search which has so often turned neutrals into enemies, was unsparingly exercised.

Whitelocke's first act in Sweden was an infringement of the law of nations. He captured a Dutch vessel on the way, and took it into the neutral port of Gottenburg.

The memory of Grotius was too firmly established in Sweden for such an act to be tolerated.

The authorities at Gottenburg protested against

* Pepys, Vol. II. p. 295.

the illegal proceeding, and Whitelocke very reluctantly discharged his prize.

One of the Senators, named Bundt, had a conversation with him shortly afterwards, about the sovereignty claimed by England in the narrow seas, when Whitelocke shrewdly suggested that notwithstanding their abstract opinions, the Swedes would hold to the *Mare Clausum* in the Baltic, if their Queen became mistress of the Sound.

Whitelocke arrived at Upsala the 20th of December, 1653, and two days afterwards was presented to the Queen.

" On entering the room, Whitelocke put off his hat, and then the Queen put off her cap, after the fashion of men, and came two or three steps forward upon the foot carpet. Her habit was of plain grey stuff, her petticoat reached to the ground, over that was a jacket such as men wear, of the same stuff, reaching to her knees ; on her left side, tied with crimson ribbon, she wore the jewel of the order of Amaranta. A black scarf was about her neck, tied before with a black ribbon, as soldiers and marines sometimes used to wear ; her hair was braided and hung loose upon her head ; she wore a black velvet cap, lined with sables, and turned up after the fashion of the country, which she used to put off and on as men used to do their hats.

"Her countenance was sprightly, but somewhat pale; she had much of majesty in her demeanour, and though her person was of the smaller size, yet her mien and carriage were very noble."

Whitelocke soon won his way into the Queen's favour; he had a quaint humour, which amused her, and he seldom had an interview without much "drollery" passing between them. The republican sometimes managed in his own way to convey a compliment. One day they were talking about the Sound dues, when Christina gave some broad hints that her navy was not in an efficient state, because she was greatly in want of money. Whitelocke turned the subject by saying that she did not waste much in fine clothes. The Queen said she certainly did not much care for dress, especially when she was in the country; and Whitelocke replied that her wearing plain clothes made them rich.

Although he was not empowered to offer subsidies, Whitelocke held out an inducement for her co-operation about the Sound, by hinting that the castles there should be put into good hands (meaning her own), as soon as they were taken from Denmark.

Oxenstiern observed that Sweden and England were not equal in this matter, as the former had already a free passage through the Sound, and if she went to war with Denmark on this question, it would be for the sole advantage of England; but Whitelocke said, very justly, that if the ships of other nations could not frequent her ports, Sweden would derive little advantage from her own privileges.

Before Whitelocke had been a month in Sweden, the Queen told him, as a great secret, of her intention to abdicate. He thought, at first, that she was " drolling " with him, but as soon as he found she was in earnest, he told her a sort of parable of an old English gentleman, who had been persuaded to give up his estate to his son. The writings were prepared, and the witnesses present to see the deed legally executed. In the meantime, the old gentleman was smoking in the parlour, when the son came in and desired his father to smoke in the kitchen, that he might not spit in the parlour. He obeyed in silence, and presently the son re-

turned to say that the deeds were all ready for him
to sign.   The old man replied that he had changed
his mind, and intended to keep his estate.   On
being asked the reason of this sudden alteration,
he said that he was determined to spit in the parlour as long as he lived.   Christina was amused
at the homely story, but said that in her case
to be quit of the crown would be to spit in the
parlour.

There was now an Ambassador from Spain at
Stockholm who was in high favour with Christina, to the great annoyance of the French party.
It was natural that the influence of France should
be paramount, so long as the war lasted, and the
French arms and subsidies were employed in
favour of Sweden.   After the peace was declared
it was Christina's policy to cultivate friendly relations with the other powers of Europe, though
not in any way to slight her old ally.

Her French courtiers were, however, highly exasperated when she extended that favour to others
which they had learned to consider their own
peculiar right.   All the most atrocious calumnies
uttered against her proceeded from this party.

Many of these libels were so extravagant and

absurd as to be unworthy of notice, and the most plausible are two anonymous productions called "Portrait de Christine," and "Adieux des François à la Suède," published at Cologne in 1668.

She is here accused of impiety because she allowed pictures to remain in the churches, which represented scripture characters without drapery, and because she used to travel with a doctor in her suite, but no chaplain.*

The author goes on to say that her conversation was so dissolute as to make him blush, but as there is strong reason to think that such a phenomenon was a physical impossibility with a French courtier of the seventeenth century, this statement may help to discredit the rest of his account.

The writer of the " Portrait de la Reine Christine" describes her as little and crooked, fickle and insincere. These are evidently exaggerations, as well as his statement that she spoke contemptuously of the Bible. The author, however, seems compelled, in spite of himself, to bear witness to her talent; for he says, " I proclaim aloud that I consider Christina the most extraordinary person in the world. I confess that her conversation is

* Adieux des François a la Suède. P. 74.

adorable, and corresponding to her intellect, to enjoy which there is no labour, fatigue, or journey that I would not undertake."*

The cause of all his hostility appears from his abuse of Pimentelle, the Spanish Ambassador, and of Bourdelot, who, though a Frenchman, was devoted to the Spanish party.

One of the special charges against her was for giving Pimentelle a costly ring at a ball, just before he returned to Spain : but the precise Whitelocke, who was an eye-witness, describes everything as being done " genteelly and without the smallest scandal or offence."

It was her custom to give handsome presents to foreign Ambassadors when they took leave; Chanut and Whitelocke himself each received a present that was probably as valuable, though not so elegant, in the form of 200lbs. of copper, which

---

* ' Elle est tout-à-fait impie, et parle de la Bible comme d'une bagatelle : à la reserve des cantiques de Salomon, qui sont, dit-elle, pleins de douceur.' Le Portrait de la Reine Christine. P. 37.

' Against this statement must be placed the fact that she gave the Finns their first translation of the Bible.' Hender_son's 'Biblical Researches and Travels in Russia.' Lon : 1836. P. 8.

was then worth about £2,500; and besides this she gave Whitelocke her picture set in diamonds.

Whitelocke describes the entertainment as a masque, in which the Queen herself took a part. At one time she was dressed as a Moorish lady, and after that she appeared as a citizen's wife. A variety of dances were performed; but though the characters were changed the men's parts were always taken by men, and the women's parts by women.

" The whole design was to show the vanity and folly of all professions and worldly things, lively represented by the exact properties and mute actions, genteelly, without the least offence or scandal.

" It held two hours : and after the dances the Queen caused her chair to be brought near to Whitelocke, where she sat down and discoursed with him of the masque. He (according to his judgment) commended it, and the inoffensiveness of it, and rare properties fitted to every representation, with the excellent performance of their parts by all, especially by the Moorish lady and the citizen's wife : at which the Queen smiled, and said she was glad he liked it.

" He replied that any of his countrymen might have been present at it without any offence, and he thanked Her Majesty for the honour she gave him to be present at it.

" When the Queen had acted the Moorish lady she retired into a room to put off her disguise: Pimentelle being there she gave him her vizor, in the mouth whereof was a diamond ring, which shined and glistened gloriously by the torch and candle light as the Queen danced: this she bade Pimentelle to keep till she called for it. Pimentelle told her he wondered she would trust a jewel of that value in the hands of a soldier: she said she would bear the adventure of it. When the masque was ended Pimentelle offered the ring again to the Queen, who told him that he had not kept it according to her commands, which were, till she called for it, which she had not yet done, nor intended as long as she lived, but that he should keep it as a memorial of her favour."*

This was the famous story of the ring which her enemies represented to have been a love-token. Pimentelle's presence in the ante-chamber was occasioned by the fact that he had taken his

* Whitelocke's Journal, 8th April, 1654.

official leave of the Queen, so that according to etiquette he could not take any part in the masque.

Pimentelle was a thorough courtier, and would have been agreeable to the Queen, even if it had not been her policy to be on friendly terms with Spain. At his first presentation, in August, 1652, he devised a refined piece of flattery. He affected to be so overcome with awe as to be unable to speak, and after a deep reverence he withdrew. A few days later he was granted an audience, when he accounted for his strange behaviour by saying that it was caused by the Queen's majestic appearance.

It is not to Christina's credit that she was deceived by such an artifice, but Pimentelle was at once received into her favour.

The object of his mission was to detach Sweden from her close and exclusive alliance with France, and to obtain for Spain a share of the trade in salt, which had been hitherto monopolized by Portugal. Pimentelle brought a quantity of salt with him for presents, and for the purpose of showing that it was of good quality.

Sweden has always been dependent on other countries for that production, and has suffered much when any interruption of the trade has occurred, for not only does she possess no salt mines, but the Baltic Sea is so slightly impregnated, that a supply cannot be procured from its waters.

Pimentelle made overtures to Whitelocke for a triple alliance between Sweden, Spain, and England, but the latter said that he had no authority to entertain such proposals, and suggested that the difference of religion might be an obstacle. The project was dropped, although the Queen was in favour of it.

She spoke much about the severity of the republican government to Catholics, and said that those who stood so much for liberty themselves, should allow liberty to others.

It was thought at this time, that her liberality was only an instance of her general spirit of toleration, and not that it was caused by any sympathy for the Catholics, although she had for a considerable period contemplated joining the Roman Church. The Jesuits kept her secret, and few persons had any suspicion of the truth.

Godeau, the Catholic Bishop of Grasse, did not receive much encouragement when he sounded her upon the subject. He was a man of considerable learning and taste, and was one of the chief founders of the French Academy. He was in frequent correspondence with Christina, who esteemed his talents.

In 1652, she wrote him a very complimentary letter, in which she expressed her gratification at receiving praise from one who was so worthy of praise himself; but she told him that the wishes which he expressed for her conversion, did not meet her approval, and she could not permit him to hope for an event which could never happen. She was convinced that she believed the things which ought to be believed, and she hoped that in due time so enlightened a man as Godean would turn to the true religion.

About the same time, she wrote to dissuade Prince Frederick of Hesse from becoming a Roman Catholic, which it was feared he would do, after the example of his brother. She said, "I will not treat the subject as it is done in colleges and pulpits; I will put aside the disputes of your Doctors with the Roman Church; I will speak to you as a disinterested person, and will only touch on one point, which is that of honour.

"You must be aware how much converts are

hated by those whom they leave, and you must know from many famous examples, that they are despised by those whom they join. Consider how the belief in his constancy affects the reputation of a Prince, and be assured that your fame will suffer if you commit such a fault."*

Christina showed in these letters a degree of insincerity which is not uncommon with those who are on the eve of changing their religion.

It will be difficult to arrive at the real motives for her conversion, but it is impossible to put forth any suppositions which are further from the truth than those which attribute it to thoughtlessness and levity. Besides her usual studious habits, there is some positive evidence to indicate the reasons by which she was actuated.

She was bewildered in a labyrinth of religious and metaphysical subjects.

" She was brought to doubt whether any true difference existed between good actions and bad, freely performed, unless, as one might be beneficial to the world, and the other injurious, which would decide their nature. She doubted also of Divine Providence, its regard or indifference to

* Archenholtz. Tome I. P. 218.

human actions; and as to the Divine Will, whether it required a certain worship and settled faith. There was no author of repute who had written on these subjects, whom she did not examine: no man eminently learned in these matters through the Northern lands, with whom she did not seek to converse; and she was inclined meanwhile to think that it was sufficient to follow in public the religion of one's country, and for the rest to live according to nature. Finally, she came to this opinion: That God, the best of beings, would be rather the worst of tyrants, if He had crucified the whole human race by bitter stings of conscience which were yet false; if, after giving to mortals the common idea that their sacrifices are pleasing to Him, and their vows accepted, He were to render no regard to these things. She was particularly struck by a passage in Cicero, 'On the Nature of the Gods,' that there could not be more than one true religion, but that all might be false, and she pondered over this for many days."*

Sceptics of this class should not be confounded

* Vita, attione, ed operatione di Alessandro VII. Opera del Card. Pallavicini.—Apud Ranke.

with scoffers. They long for truth, and when they find that reason cannot give them satisfaction, they embrace the religion which allows the least exercise of it, as if in revenge for its shortcomings.

The antagonism of reason and faith is not confined to hostile sects ; it frequently operates in the same individuals, and they are the victims alternately of doubt and superstition, like Lord Herbert of Cherbury, who, when he had finished his. book against all revelation, actually prayed for some supernatural sign to know whether he should publish it.*

Such a frame of mind has ever been found favourable to the adoption of Roman Catholic doctrines, and their effect on a candid mind has been admirably described by a great writer, who says : " It is not strange that wise men, weary of investigation, and longing to believe something, and yet seeing objections to everything, should submit themselves absolutely to teachers who, with firm and undoubting faith, lay claim to a supernatural commission. Thus we frequently see inquisitive and restless spirits take refuge from their own scepticism in the bosom of a church

* Mosheim, Vol. III., p. 428.

which pretends to infallibility, and after questioning the existence of a Deity, bring themselves to worship a wafer."*

It was while Christina's mind was in this state of unwilling scepticism that the Portuguese Ambassador, Pareira, arrived in Stockholm, with a confessor and a chaplain in his suite, who were both Jesuits.†

Their names were Macedo and Andrada. The former was a man of some learning; he was bold, prudent, and zealous, and had already distinguished himself as a missionary among the heathen in Africa.

Don Joseph Pinto Pareira was no scholar, and his rank was his chief recommendation for the office of ambassador. He was ignorant of Latin, which was then the language of diplomacy, and was obliged to employ Macedo as an interpreter. The Jesuit soon discovered that Christina spoke respectfully of the Pope, and determined to take advantage of so promising a symptom. He carried on theological arguments with her in the presence

---

* Macaulay's History of England, Vol IV., p. 28.

† Galeazzo Gualdo, 'Historia della sacra Real Maesta di Christina,' &c.—Roma, 1656.

of his chief, who believed the conversations were all about politics.

Pareira was to return to Portugal in September, 1651, and his approaching departure induced Christina to take some more decided steps.

On the 12th of August, she led Macedo into a private apartment, and told him that she wished to disclose a secret of great importance.

She said that he was the first Jesuit she had ever known, but that she felt confidence in his prudence and fidelity ; and she requested him to get two Italians of his order sent to Sweden. They were to be intelligent and accomplished men, and, to avoid suspicion, they were to come in the character of two private gentlemen travelling for amusement.

Macedo undertook to convey a letter from Christina to Piccolomini, the General of the Jesuits, and he swore to observe secrecy.

The ambassador had no inkling of what was going on. Macedo asked his permission to take a little journey to Hamburg, but was refused. The Jesuit related his difficulty to the Queen, who recommended him to go at once without leave.

Macedo had some trouble in making his escape,

and was obliged to pass the night upon a rock, where he was waiting for a vessel.

At the demand of the ambassador, a man-of-war was sent after the truant confessor, with orders to arrest him; but the captain had private counter-orders from the Queen that he was not to find the object of his search.

Poor Macedo was proclaimed a rogue and a villain; and it was even said that he had turned Lutheran, and had taken a wife with him. In the meantime he arrived safely at Rome, where he found that Piccolomini was dead. His successor, Gosnino Nikel, received the Queen's letter, and entered warmly into the scheme.

Exercising that marvellous authority which is independent of political or geographical limits, he chose Francesco Malines, professor of theology at Turin, and Paolo Casati, professor of mathematics at Rome, to undertake the adventure.

The emissaries were both men of integrity and learning. They obeyed the order to start immediately for Sweden, and would have done the same if they had been chosen for service among the Pagans of China or the savages of North America. Their mission to Sweden was hardly less dangerous, for their lives would have been forfeited if their errand had been discovered.

They reached Stockholm in March, 1652, and their disguise was so well preserved that it was not penetrated even by Christina.

They travelled from Hamburg with the Senator Rosenhane, and ingratiated themselves with him so much that he presented them at Court, though quite unconscious of what he was doing.

It was not until Christina had seen them several times, that she suspected who they were. She then spoke to Casati in a low tone, and said : " Perhaps you have letters for me." Casati replied in the affirmative without even turning his head, and the Queen added, " Do not name them to any one."

The next day they had a private audience, and Christina soon began to propound startling questions.

They came prepared with arguments to prove the superiority of their own Church, but Christina asked whether there was any true difference between good and evil, or whether all was determined by the utility or injurious character of the action ; how doubts with regard to the existence of a Providence were to be set at rest; whether the soul of man were really immortal?

To such questions as these, a dry assumption of the Church's authority would have been no answer. The Jesuits were educated and intelligent men, who did not attempt to offer mathematical evidence of the unseen world. They used the finer arguments of analogy, and above all they insisted that " those parts of religion which were beyond the reach of reason, were nowise opposed to reason."

Although it may be difficult with such weapons to gain a formal victory over a captious antagonist, it is easier to satisfy a candid and intellectual inquirer. Christina appeared to have received a reasonable solution of her doubts, for she passed on to the dogmas of the Roman Catholic Church, and demurred, as might have been expected, at the invocation of saints, and the veneration of images and relics. She frequently returned to the subject, but the final success of the Jesuits seemed doubtful, for she sometimes told them that they had better return home, as the attempt they were making was impracticable, because she thought she could never become wholly a Catholic at heart.

They were agreeably surprised one day by her question, " What would you say if I were nearer to becoming a Catholic than you suppose ? "

She asked at the same time whether the Pope could not grant her a dispensation to receive the Lord's Supper, once in the year, according to the Lutheran rites.

Such a concession would have robbed the Jesuits of the whole honour of their victory, and they replied that the Pope could not do so. " Then," said Christina, " there is no help, I must resign the crown."

Casati was sent to give an account of her intentions to the Pope, and her only confidant in Sweden was Pimentelle.

It is impossible to consider Christina's conversion without giving some attention to the general state of religion during the 17th century.

In the two ages which have since elapsed, such great changes have taken place, that the ensuing remarks will not apply to the present time, and a Protestant may now venture to do justice to the Catholics of two hundred years ago.

At that time the two great faults of the Roman Church, ambition and intolerance, were equalled or surpassed by the Protestants. These faults were more glaring when contrasted with some apparent improvement in the Catholics. The finances of the Papacy supplied vast sums for ecclesiastical buildings, for the conversion of the heathen, for the support of new religious orders whose objects were praiseworthy and charitable—to educate the poor, and to tend the sick. The Protestants adopted the system which had so long been a reproach to their antagonists; they made religion an excuse for political movements. The German princes who adopted the Reformed faith hardly attempted to conceal that their chief motive was to gain possession of the rich Catholic Bishoprics.

The French Huguenot nobles sought, under the same pretext, to render themselves independent of all superior authority. Under a shallow guise of religious enthusiasm they aimed at anarchy: and in their occasional reconciliations with their government they always insisted on keeping a number of fortresses in their hands, from which they treated with their Sovereign as with an enemy. The English Puritans had more genuine religious feeling, yet as Christina shrewdly observed to Whitelocke, "there were men among them who made profession of more holiness than was in them, hoping for advantage by it."

Passing over the divine maxims of charity and love contained in the Gospel which the Catholics were in some degree acting upon, the Reformers dwelt upon the sanguinary examples of the Old Testament. The old intolerance of the Roman Church was imitated by sects whose leading doctrine was freedom of opinion, and whose very existence was built on that foundation.

One of our greatest champions, Chillingworth, felt that this intolerance was illogical as well as unjust, when he said that "Protestants were inexcusable if they did violence to other men's consciences." Many good men were disgusted at the inordinate pretensions and acrimonious disputes of the different Protestant sects, and could not deny that the Catholic Church, at least in theory, was more consistent.

The faults of the Protestants combined with the efforts of the Catholics to bring a number of converts to the Roman Church about the middle of the seventeenth century, and it is remarkable that a large proportion of these were men of more than ordinary abilities. The balance of power

established between the rival communions facili-
tated this result, for generous minds naturally
revolt from conversions which may be imputed to
fear.

The victorious career of the Swedes enabled
Protestants to change their religion without being
branded as cowards. Many of the converts were
professors at the Protestant universities, and their
example naturally produced imitators. The learned
Lambecius, Professor of History, and Rector of
the University of Hamburg, concealed his conversion for some years.* Morin, the greatest Hebrew
scholar of his time, went over openly.†

Gaudentius, a professor of reputation at Pisa,
joined the Roman Church from conviction.‡

Nicholas Stenon, the most eminent Danish
physician of his time, did the same. He made
important additions to anatomical knowledge, and
gave his name to a part of the human frame of
which he discovered the functions (*ductus Stenon-
ianus*). He also made important observations on
the nervous system, and the structure of the

---

* Huet's Memoirs, Vol. I., p. 110.
† Hallam, ' Lit. of Europe.' Vol. III., p. 223.
‡ Naudeana.

brain. He did not limit his researches to subjects connected with his own profession, but took some steps towards founding the modern science of geology.

The fossil bones and shells contained in rocks had been hitherto pronounced the work of chance, or of the stars; Stenon proclaimed their vital origin, although he qualified this step in advance by supposing that remains so deeply imbedded owed their position to the deluge.*

In Stenon's case, at least, his change of religion is to be deplored, for by its means a great interpreter of Nature was converted to a priest, a missionary, and an ascetic.

Pfeiffer and Blumius were two eminent professors who joined the Roman Church.† A more celebrated man than either of them was Holsteinius, a native of Hamburg, who was in communication with nearly all the most learned men in Europe. He renounced the Protestant communion, and took up his residence at Rome, where he became librarian of the Vatican.

Grotius, as already related, was on the point of

* Biographie Universelle.—Richardson's Geology, p. 31.
† Mosheim. Vol. III., p. 486.

becoming a Catholic, and the learned Casaubon appears to have held very nearly the same religious opinions as Grotius.

The defections among those remarkable for their rank were equally numerous. Among the most distinguished were Wolfgang William, Count Palatine of the Rhine; Christian William, Marquis of Brandenburg; Ernest, Prince of Hesse; John Frederick, Duke of Brunswick; and Frederick Augustus, King of Poland.

Many others of less note might be added to this list, as, for example, Henrietta de Coligni, Countess de Suze, grand-daughter of the victim of St. Bartholemew's Day. She was on bad terms with the Count de Suze, who was a Protestant, and Christina said, satirically, that she had changed her faith to avoid meeting her husband either in the present world, or in the world to come.*

Christina's conversion was so strange an event, that all kinds of surmises have been made as to its cause. An opinion very generally advanced was, that she did not think of changing her religion until after she had made up her mind to abdicate,

* Voltaire. 'Siecle de Louis XIV.' P. 593

and that her only motive was to secure a good reception in those countries which she intended to visit. It is probable that this consideration had some weight, but it is reasonable to suppose that other causes concurred in bringing about the result.

The biographer of Descartes asserts roundly that the honour of her conversion was due to that philosopher.* Pimentelle, Bourdelot, and others were supposed to have had a share in the work ; and as Christina had studied the subject deeply, it seems unfair to assume that conviction had nothing to do with the change, merely because she did not show herself to be an enthusiastic or a bigoted Catholic.

Whitelocke does not appear to have had any suspicions of the Queen's religious opinions, but he was shocked at the pictures, images, and crucifixes displayed in the Lutheran churches, and still more so at the Queen's custom of giving balls on Sundays, a custom which, in a spirit of true charity, she altered, when she found how much offence it gave to the English Ambassador.

Christina expressed great admiration of Crom-

* Baillet, 'Vie de Descartes.' Tome II. p. 433.

well, and compared him to her ancestor, Gustavus
Vasa.. She at one time entertained the idea of
visiting England, but the Protector gave her no
encouragement, partly from political reasons, and
partly, it was said, on account of the jealousy of
his wife.*

The Queen generally mixed up some " drollery "
in her conversations with the English Minister ;
she used to speak about the chief notables in
England, the Duke of Buckingham, the Earl of
Arundel, Mr. Selden, and others'; and showed such
accurate knowledge of that country, that Whitelocke said, " One would have imagined that England had been her native country, so well was she
furnished with the characters of most persons
there of consideration, and with the story of the
nation."†

Christina exercised so much influence on the
Puritan, as to induce him to dance with her at a
ball which she gave on the occasion of a marriage
between Baron Horn and a lady of the Sparre
family. By his own account he acquitted himself

* Guizot's Life of Cromwell.
† Whitelocke. P. 284.

very well, for when he led the Queen back to her seat, she exclaimed in her abrupt manner—" Par Dieu, these Hollanders are lying fellows ; they reported to me that all the noblesse of England were of the King's party, and none but mechanics of the Parliament party, and not a gentleman among them ; now I thought to try you, and to shame you if you could not dance ; but I see that you are a gentleman, and have been bred a gentleman."

The bride and bridegroom were obliged to march about in procession, and the ball had already lasted until two in the morning, when Whitelocke, in his quaint way, told the Senator Bundt that the Queen was a tyrant to detain the newly married couple so late. Bundt repeated the joke to Christina, who laughed heartily, and at the same time ordered the dancing to cease, upon which the bridegroom came and thanked Whitelocke for his " seasonable drollery."*

One of the most important ceremonies was performed the next day, when, according to the Swedish custom, the husband gave his wife her dowry. The whole court was assembled, and

* Whitelocke. P. 173.

Senator Bundt proclaimed aloud the amount that was settled on the bride.*

Twelve witnesses, or trustees, engaged to see the money properly disposed of, and each in his turn laid his hand on a silver-headed spear which was held by the bridegroom.

The spear was then laid at the bride's feet, and was finally thrown out of the window, to be scrambled for by the people.

It was a long time before the treaty was concluded between Sweden and England. Oxenstiern interposed delays, because he doubted the stability of the English Government, but the treaty was signed at last on the 11th of April, 1654.

It provided that there should be a good, sincere, firm peace and correspondence between the Queen and kingdom of Sweden, and the Protector and Commonwealth of England; that each should advance the common profit, and should admonish the other of any conspiracy or machination of enemies, and that neither should do anything to the detriment of the other.

* This was called the ' Morgeng gaven' (morning's gift), and the term is used in the English law to signify a second dowry.

Both the contracting parties were to endeavour, with all candour and affection, to remove the hindrances which had hitherto interrupted the liberty of navigation and commerce between the two nations.

Subjects of one of the States were free to travel through all the territories of the other, without any safe conduct or passport, either general or special; and each might buy from or export to the other all kinds' of merchandize, including arms and provisions of war.

The eleventh article said, " Although it be prohibited by the former articles of this league and friendship, that either of the confederates shall give aid or assistance to the enemies of the other, nevertheless, it is no way to be understood that it is denied to the confederate, who is not at war, to have commerce and navigation with the enemies of that confederate who is at war."

These articles had all been discussed by Christina personally, and the last mentioned one bears evidence of her wise and statesmanlike views.

In politics as well as in knowledge her attention was not confined to any particular subjects, to the exclusion of the rest. She had the same intimate acquaintance with other countries as with England and France, and her good will was extended to regions from whence she certainly could have no reciprocal benefits to expect. She wrote a friendly letter to the King of Abyssinia : she expressed her admiration at the Christian religion being preserved in his dominions, although surrounded by its enemies, and she exhorted him to hold fast that divine faith.*

Russia at this time showed little sign of her future greatness, but frequent intercourse took place between the Swedish and Russian governments. The embassies of the latter were remarkable for their barbaric magnificence.

Chanut mentions the Queen giving audience to some Russian ambassadors, who entered her presence with ninety servants carrying pieces of cloth of gold before them. They read their speeches, and an interpreter gave a literal translation line by line. The Czar's letter was wrapped in black crape, but when the Chancellor advanced to take it, the Ambassadors abruptly refused to give it him, and handed it to the Queen themselves.*

† Archenholtz. Vol. I., p. 352.
† Chanut. P. 39.

After the Peace of Westphalia, the Swedish Government entertained the idea of extending their territory on the side of Russia, but the Czar made an effort in 1650 to gain the friendship of Christina, and agreed to pay a considerable sum of money in compensation for the Swedish peasants who had fled from their own country to take refuge in Russia.

This concession was just in time to save him some trouble, for the following year Tartar envoys arrived in Stockholm, who were sent to urge Christina to take hostile measures against the Czar: their advice was declined, in consequence of the recent negotiations with Russia.

Among the most favourably received of Christina's courtiers were some refugees who had no scruple about giving her important information.

One of these was Corfitz Ulfeld, who was married to the late King of Denmark's favourite daughter.

After the death of Christian, his son and successor, Frederick III., showed great hostility towards Ulfeld. It was said that the opinions of the latter were too democratic to please the Danish monarch. He was also accused of being too attentive to one of the King's mistresses, and even of attempting his Sovereign's life.

To save his own life, he was obliged to fly, and his wife, then in an interesting condition, accompanied him, disguised as a page.

They made their escape to a ship, and were about to sail, when the page unfortunately took a fancy to some cherries which she had seen in the town. According to the notions then prevalent, her life would have been endangered by a disappointment, and Ulfeld gallantly went on shore again in quest of the cherries. His expedition was successful, and he had the satisfaction of bringing the fruit to his wife.

The fugitives were well received by Christina, to the great annoyance of the Danish King, who represented to her that, among Ulfeld's misdemeanours, he had received a sum of 24,000 dollars for the use of the exiled King of England, of which Charles Stuart declared he had never received a fraction.

Christina replied, "Ulfeld is an honourable gentleman, and cannot have done anything so base. If he says he has given the so-called King of England 24,000 dollars, I believe that he has done so, and if the King of England denies it. he lies : if twelve such Kings as he were to deny it, I would say they all twelve lie."*

On further investigation it was proved that Christina was right in her estimate of Charles II.—and of Ulfeld. It was ascertained that the latter had furnished arms to Montrose to the value of 36,000 dollars, and thus, so far from robbing the distressed monarch, he had actually paid for him 12,000 dollars more than he had received.

Ulfeld continued to show the most inveterate hostility towards his brother-in-law and Sovereign; he gave Christina information of all the weak points in Denmark, descriptions of the fortified places, returns of the troops, and lists of the disaffected officers.

He urged Christina to invade his country; and it is a curious fact that the vindictiveness of another refugee, named Radziejousky, caused the project to fail.

This man was a refugee from Poland, and he betrayed the intentions of Sweden to the Danish Government, because he wished Christina to attack his own country instead, and he thought she

* Fryxell, Nionde Delen. Tjugesjunde Kapitlet.

would be more likely to invade Poland, if Denmark appeared to be on her guard.

Radziejowsky had been Chancellor of Poland, and his wife, who was very beautiful, was suspected of too great intimacy with the King, John Casimir.

During her husband's absence, she left his house and took refuge in a convent.

On his return, Radziejowsky collected five hundred retainers, and attempted to storm the convent; but the lady's brothers defended the place, and the assailants were repulsed with heavy loss. Radziejowsky then fled to Stockholm, and Christina naturally sheltered a man who could give her so much information about her enemies in Poland.

It was during the residence of Ulfeld and Radziejowsky at Stockholm, that Christina founded her whimsical order of Amaranta.

Early in 1653, she gave a grand *fête*, which was called the Festival of the Gods, and which represented how the gods and goddesses were received on earth by shepherds and shepherdesses.

The Swedes were much offended that all the gods were represented by foreigners, so that the

allegory was interpreted to signify the conde-
scension of those illustrious individuals in visiting
the barbarous North.

Ulfeld, Pimentelle, and Radziejowsky represented
Jupiter, Mars, and Bacchus; Christina herself
appeared as a shepherdess, although she rather
inconsistently wore a costly dress, blazing with
diamonds. The dancing continued until six in the
morning, when all the company resumed their
own dresses, and Christina distributed her jewels
among them, in remembrance of the pleasure
they had had together. If the matter had terminated here, it would not have been much more
irrational than a modern fancy-ball.

Unfortunately, Christina determined to insti-
tute an order in memory of an event insignificant
in itself, which recorded no great actions, and ap-
pealed to no elevated sentiments, and only commemorated an act of singular profusion and extravagance.

It is true that the circumstances which attended the foundation of our own highest order
of Knighthood were not more dignified, but men
reasoned less on such subjects in the 14th than
they did in the 17th century.

It was said, indeed, that the English order of the Garter gave Christina the idea of an order of her own. When Charles II. was in exile, he showed his bad taste by sending the Garter to Charles Gustavus.

Christina, who wished to stand well with Cromwell, refused to let the Prince accept it, and said that "she would not let any member of her flock be marked by the hand of a stranger;"* but the circumstance seems to have suggested her order of the "Amaranta."

Christina had chosen this name for herself at the *fête*; it signifies immortal, from the Greek word *Αμαραντινος*, never fading.

The new order consisted of fifteen ladies and fifteen gentlemen, and they all dined with the Queen at one of her country houses every Saturday. The rules were not less fanciful than the origin of the Amaranta.

The Queen, seated on her throne, received the intended Knight, who was supported by his godfathers in chivalry. The aspirant knelt and swore between the Queen's hands, to be faithful and to maintain the interests of the Order. Those who

* Ranke's History of the Popes. Vol. II., p. 357.

were unmarried, swore that they would never marry; those who were already married, swore that they would not contract the bonds of wedlock a second time. After the administration of the oath, they were invested with the insignia, which was made of gold and diamonds, and represented a double AA intertwined, and a band with the inscription, "Dolce nella memoria."

The special motto was embroidered on a ribbon worn round the neck, and if Christina had desired to satirize herself she could hardly have done so more effectually than by the words "Semper eadem."

The institution gave rise to various scandals. Pimentelle's name was Antonio, and the double A was supposed to be emblematic of Amaranta and Antonio.

The name itself was said to derive its origin from a town named Amaranta in Portugal, where Pimentelle's property was situated.

Whitelocke gives rather a different account of the order of the Amaranta. He omits the absurd conditions relating to matrimony, and merely states that the knight knelt before the Queen, held up his hands between her hands, and swore to defend virtue, and the honour of virtuous ladies; to endeavour to correct vice : to perform honourable actions, and to keep his faith inviolable.*

Whitelocke says that the double A was emblematic of the first and last letter of Amaranta, and that the name itself belonged to a certain noble and famous lady, who was an eminent pattern and example of the highest honour and virtue. Unfortunately he has left no means of verifying his assertion, as he did not say when and where this lady flourished.

It must not be forgotten, however, that Whitelocke himself was a Knight of the Amaranta, and it seems very improbable that he would have sworn to observe conditions which would not only have interfered with his liberty of action, but would have reflected on his own previous conduct in marrying three times.

It would appear that these conditions were either omitted in Whitelocke's case, or else that these absurdities, like many others of which Christina was accused, were inventions of her enemies.

In considering Christina's abdication and conversion, it is not easy to determine which was the cause, and which the effect.

* Whitelocke's Journal. 16th February.

She would probably never have openly renounced the Protestant faith so long as she wore the crown of Sweden, but at the same time there is great doubt whether the various causes which led to her abdication would have been sufficient unless she had already been secretly inclined to become a Catholic.

It has already been mentioned that, when she retracted her first determination to abdicate, she did so with the intention of carrying it out at a future time.

The reasons which led to her resolution continued to exist, and fresh reasons had arisen.

The military glory of Sweden, and her own reputation for genius and learning, had raised her to a degree of celebrity at which her fame could hardly remain stationary, and it could only be increased by some great actions of her own; yet her energies were already weakened by too great and too early application, and by the idolatry of which the most eminent men in Europe made her the object.

The state of the finances was not improved, but the minds of the Swedes were still directed towards war. Christina not only disliked war for its own sake, she also felt that it might cause her to hold a place in the estimation of the people, inferior to that of a successful general, especially if that general was the next heir to the throne. The military glory of Sweden could scarcely rise higher. But it might be tarnished by a single reverse, and Christina would share more largely in the disgrace of an unfortunate general, than she could ever do in the fame of a victorious one. Such an extraordinary act as her abdication when at the height of her glory, might constitute a fresh claim to the admiration which had become almost necessary to her existence. It would relieve her from cares which had become, intolerably irksome, and might save her from forfeiting the esteem she had once enjoyed.

The final decision cost her a severe struggle, for contrary to her usual character, Christina was now silent, melancholy, and absent.

In January, 1654, Chanut made a last attempt to change her resolution, but this effort was feebler than before. He said, "Madam, Whilst the report is so generally spread that your Majesty is about to resign the government of your kingdom, it is impossible for me to argue about it with calm-

ness and indifference, as if it were simply a
political problem, neither can I remain silent when
your honour and glory are concerned.

" I confess my weakness, Madam, but I confess
it without shame, since I find that all those who
most honour your Majesty, speak with dread of so
extraordinary a design. I am overwhelmed with
astonishment and fear, when I consider what will
be the result of such a resolution, although I am
reassured by two considerations. One of these is,
that your Majesty knows yourself, and everything
else, better than we do ; the other is, that I recollect your Majesty has told me that you would
always submit your actions to Divine Providence,
which watches over all those who do so, and directs
their counsels in such a way that the results are
always fortunate. The only change I apprehend
is the one your Majesty is meditating ; for no
change can take place in my devotion and respect.
My obligations are independent of time and place ;
there can be no alteration except concerning the
manner in which your Majesty may be pleased
to try my obedience, which can neither diminish
nor increase in its zeal and fidelity."

* Archenholtz. P. 395.

Christina's answer to the old diplomatist's letter was earnest and impetuous, and the sentiments she expressed were wild, and sometimes false. She said : " I have already explained to you the reasons which make me persevere in my intention to abdicate.

" You know this whim has lasted a long time, and that I have only resolved to carry it out after eight years' reflection. It is five years since I communicated my intention to you, and I saw then that it was only your sincere affection, and the interest which you took in my fortunes, that made you oppose reasons which you could not blame. I was pleased to see that you saw nothing unworthy of me in these reasons.

" You know what I told you the last time we conversed on this subject. I have not changed during the interval, and all my actions have been directed with the same aim. I am ready to finish my acting, and to retire behind the scenes; I do not trouble myself about applause. The part which I have performed was not composed according to the ordinary laws of the theatre. What is strong and vigorous does not always please.

" I allow every one to judge me according to

their capacity, and although it is true I cannot hinder them, yet I would not do so if I had the power.

"I know that few will judge me favourably, but I feel satisfied that you will be among the number.

"Others are ignorant of my reasons, and of my feelings, for I have never explained myself except to you, and to one other friend whose mind is noble and refined enough to judge as you will do. ' Sufficit unus, sufficit nullus.'

"Those who examine this action according to the maxims which commonly prevail will certainly blame it, but I will never take the trouble to make my apology to them.

"In the leisure which I am preparing for myself I shall never be so idle as to think of them. I shall employ it in examining my past life, and in correcting my faults without being surprised at them, and without repenting of them.

"I shall have pleasure in the remembrance of the worthy men I have benefited, as well as in the recollection that I have punished sternly those who deserved punishment.

"It will be my consolation that I have condemned no man unjustly, but on the contrary have spared some who were guilty:

" I have preferred the interests of the State to every other consideration, and have nothing to reproach myself with in the administration.

" I have possessed power without pride, and I relinquish it without regret. Do not fear for me; my wealth is beyond the power of fortune; I am happy whatever may chance.

" Yes, I am happy, and shall be happy always. I do not fear the Providence of which you speak. If it interferes in my affairs, I will submit with due respect and resignation ; but if I am permitted to conduct them myself, I will employ the talents with which Providence has blessed me, in being happy.

" I shall be happy when I believe that I have no reason to fear anything from men nor from God. I will pass the rest of my life in such thoughts, and in watching from my haven those who are still exposed to the storms of life. How many would be envious of me, if they only knew my happiness.

" You, however, have too much regard for me to be envious, and I can claim your regard, because

I will frankly confess that some of these sentiments are derived from you.

" I learned them from your conversation, and I hope some day to cultivate them at leisure with you.   I am sure you will not break your word, and that you will continue to be my friend, as I part with nothing that deserves your esteem.

&c.,   &c.,   &c.,   " CHRISTINA."

" Westerås, 28th Feb., 1654."

Chanut answered this letter, but made no further attempt to change her resolution, and in fact any such effort must have been useless, for a fortnight before he received her letter Christina had announced her intention to the assembled Senate. On the 11th of February she addressed them as follows :—

" I allowed myself to be dissuaded three years ago from abdicating the throne.

" Since that time I have reflected maturely, and have determined to adopt the course I then proposed.   There is no difficulty as regards the Prince Charles Gustavus; he has been acknowledged heir to the crown; the kingdom is due to him, and he will govern it ably.

" Many reasons lead me to resign the administration: my resolution is taken, and I will never depart from it. I do not therefore ask your opinion, but only your assistance in bringing the affair to a conclusion, and in arranging that the Prince may succeed to the throne with safety and tranquillity."

The Senate repeated the arguments they had used in 1651. They said that their oaths of allegiance had been taken unconditionally, and that she herself could not absolve them. Christina would not accept their interpretation, and adjourned the meeting until the 15th of the month, when she again announced her determination to the Senate, and told them that although her motive was then only known to God, it would not long remain a secret.* She probably alluded to her conversion, which does not appear to have been suspected by the Senate.

Count Brahe opposed her intention with considerable vehemence. He said that her abdication would be an offence to God, a violation of her own

* 'Gud kände rätta orsaken dertill: med tiden skulle den och blifva för menniskor uppenbar.'—Fryxell, Tionde Delen. P. 186.

oath, and of her people's rights, and he added that whoever had advised Her Majesty to take such a step was no honourable man, but a false knave. The Queen said that was a rash expression, since men of high rank had not only approved of her purpose, but had assisted in forwarding it.

The sturdy old nobleman replied, " I have given my opinion of them, they are welcome to take it to themselves."

Christina again hinted at some hidden cause. " If you knew," she said, "the secret reason, which as yet I must conceal, you would think my conduct less strange."

The subject was then referred to the meeting of the Diet, and Christina employed the interval in negotiations with the Prince about the revenues and privileges which she wished to reserve.

Charles Gustavus was well aware that he was indebted to Christina alone for the brilliant prospects which were opening upon him, and was profuse in the expression of his consideration and devotion. When they parted, she said, " Farewell, my cousin, when we next meet 1 shall greet you as King." Charles Gustavus took care to put no difficulties in the way, and although he professed to the last his reluctance to do anything which would .facilitate her abdication, there is little doubt that he was insincere, and that his partizans were engaged actively, although secretly, in stimulating the Queen's desire to be quit of the government.*

Christina wished to make a further disposition of the crown, in case Charles Gustavus should die without children, but the Senate would not allow her to interfere any further in the succession.

The revenues she required were very large, and she has been justly censured for desiring to retain so considerable a portion of the crown domains after she had relinquished the cares and duties of royalty. She demanded the full sovereignty as well as the revenues of the islands of Ösel, Öland, Gothland, Wollin, and Usedom, the towns of Norköping and Göteborg, and the chief part of the Swedish possessions in Pomerania.

Such a power would have enabled her at some

* 'Hans första och förnamsta afsigt var at vinna kronan, Som medel användes låtsad likgilltiget för samma kronan. ihårdig undergifvenhet mot Kristina, och, som man tror, hemliga handtlangare, hvilka oförmärkt underbläste denna sednares ovilja mot Sverge och längtan efter främmande ｜and.'—Fryxell, Tionde Delen. P. 196.

future time to sell or alienate a part of the Swedish
territory, and Christina was obliged to be content
with the revenues only of these places.   Among
these possessions were some which had been granted
to Magnus de la Gardie.   The Senate and nobles
felt that a principle was involved which concerned
themselves nearly, and they refused their consent
to have these places included in Christina's
appanage.

Her hostility to De la Gardie led her to adopt
a course which she had hitherto stigmatized as
dishonourable, and she had resort to an artifice to
overcome the opposition of the Senate and nobles,
which displayed more shrewdness than dignity.
The Senate and nobles were each assembled in
their own chamber at the same hour, when they
were visited by two of Christina's adherents, who
warned each assembly that the other had given
their consent, and that the one which held out
would become obnoxious both to the Queen and
to the States.   The result of this trick was that
they both reluctantly gave their votes in the way
the Queen desired.

The Diet met at Upsala on the 21st of May.
All the dignitaries of the kingdom, as well as the

foreign ambassadors, were present when the Queen entered the hall, and took her seat amidst profound silence.

It was the custom on such occasions for the Chancellor to advance and greet the States in the Queen's name, but the silence was prolonged, and yet Oxenstiern remained motionless. After waiting some time, Christina beckoned to him, when the Chancellor advanced, with deep reverences, and a conversation took place between them in a low tone, which was only heard by a few of those who were nearest. The substance of it was, that the old man begged to be excused from this duty. He had sworn to her father to do his utmost to maintain the crown of Sweden on her head, and this oath would be violated if he assisted by word or deed in her abdication.

He then retired to his place, and Christina also sat down again. During the short silence which ensued, she arranged her thoughts, and then stood up without any further preparation to greet the Diet herself.

She said that the purpose for which they were convoked might surprise them, but that, if they would consider what she had done for a long time, they would perceive that it was no hastily formed conclusion on her part, but an affair on which she had reflected maturely, and towards which her acts had long tended.

She reminded them of the settlement of the succession, made some years before, to which they had given their consent. She said that, during the ten years she had reigned, she had sacrificed her own inclinations to the welfare of the country; that she had spared no labour to procure the repose which they now enjoyed both at home and abroad; and that the only reward she asked for all her cares and anxieties, was their consent to her abdication. She then asked them to provide for her subsistence, about which she had already agreed with the Prince.

The spokesmen of the different orders then advanced to answer her greeting. They extolled the wisdom of her administration, and said that no prince could have ruled the country better than she had done, that no people were happier than the Swedes, and that all they wanted was to remain under her rule, and to enjoy the fruits of her wisdom.

The deputy of the peasants at least was sincere.

He approached without the number of reverences prescribed by courtly etiquette, and addressed her as follows :—

"Alas! madam, why does your Majesty think of leaving our country, and us who love you so much? What can you desire better than you have? Such a kingdom cannot easily be found again.

"Continue in your gears, good madam, and be the fore-horse as long as you live, and we will help you the best we can to bear your burden."*

The peasant then took her hand, pressed and kissed it several times, then turning his back to her, he pulled out of his pocket a dirty handkerchief, and wiped the tears from his eyes as he retired.

The Diet wished to make it a condition that Christina should reside in Sweden, because they did not like such considerable revenues to be spent out of the country; but Charles Gustavus represented that as the Queen absolutely renounced the throne and descended to a private station, she ought to have the liberty of living where she liked. The desire of pleasing his bene-

* Fryxell, p. 197.—Whitelocke, Vol. II., p. 223.

factress was not his only motive : he thought it desirable on his own account that Christina should reside abroad. He feared that if she remained in Sweden she might get tired of inactivity, and form plans to regain the power which she was now so anxious to resign.

After Christina had pronounced her address to the Diet, her formal declaration still remained to be read. Oxenstiern refused to do this, and the duty was performed by the Senator Rosenhane.

The declaration began by conveying the Queen's congratulations to the Diet, that the three scourges under which Sweden had suffered, war, pestilence, and famine, were all removed. For the two blessings of public health and plenty, she expressed her gratitude to God, and added her supplications that His chastisements might be averted in future.

The blessing of peace she also ascribed to the goodness of God, but she mentioned her own efforts to promote it with dignity and modesty.

Hostilities were not to be apprehended on the side of Russia, because her Commissioners had carefully settled the boundary questions between the countries.

The truce with Poland was agreed to for twenty-six years, and though Her Majesty would rather have announced a perpetual peace, yet she still hoped this happy result might follow the efforts of her Commissioners and mediators at Lübeck.

She rejoiced in the peace and amity with the Emperor and the Roman empire, without arrogating the merit to herself, which she might so justly have done.

The good terms Sweden was on with France and Spain, were mentioned with satisfaction, "but particularly Her Majesty rejoiceth that the perilous war made in the ocean between the powerful Commonwealths of England and the United Provinces (by which we have received very great damage in our trade throughout, as it appeareth) is appeased and ended; and that, since, Her Majesty hath made an alliance with the Commonwealth of England, for the security of navigation and commerce, so that the faithful subjects of Her Majesty may thereby hope to have great advantage and profit."

The Act of Abdication was performed on the morning of the 6th of June.

It was a melancholy spectacle.*

* Grefne P. Brahe's Tänkebok, § 92.

The Queen wore a plain white dress, over which all the ornaments of royalty were placed.

Charles Gustavus was clothed in black from head to foot. Christina sat for the last time on the silver throne, the gift of the once highly esteemed Magnus de la Gardie.

Shering Rosenhane read with a loud voice the Act by which the Queen released her subjects from their oath of fidelity, and the conditions on which she transferred the Crown to her cousin, Charles Gustavus.

The domains which she reserved were enumerated. Christina undertook to do nothing injurions to Sweden, but she was declared free from all control, and she was to have entire and absolute authority over all her retinue.

The Queen then summoned the great officers of State to take from her the emblems of royalty. The sword, the apple, and the sceptre were removed and placed on a table at her left hand, but when Brahe was desired to remove the crown from her head, he positively refused to do so, and the Queen took it off herself and placed it in his hands. The mantle was next taken off, and this was torn to pieces by those who desired a relic of their young Queen.

Christina then stood in the plain white garment and pronounced her farewell address.

She spoke with her usual eloquence, although her voice trembled occasionally, and showed how great an effort it required to restrain her tears. Few of the spectators had the same self-command, and most of them wept without control, to hear the last heir of the Vasas bid them farewell.

She said, " I thank God who raised me to be Queen over so mighty a nation, and who has given me such wonderful blessings and successes. I thank the noblemen who preserved the kingdom for me during my minority; and I thank the States for the fidelity they have shown to me.

" In difficult times, I have done nothing with which my conscience reproaches me.

" So far as my strength would let me, I sacrificed my own peace to assure your tranquillity."

She spoke of her father's great actions, and added, that in Charles Gustavus she presented them a Prince who would follow in his steps.

She begged them to show the same fidelity to her successor which they had ever shown to her. She now released them from their oath, and thanked them from her heart for their truth and obedience.

She then turned to the Prince, and her voice was firmer as she reminded him of the glory of his predecessors, and exhorted him to prove himself worthy of them.

It was, she said, because she recognized the same great qualities in him, and not merely on account of their relationship, that she had chosen him as her successor. The only proof she asked of his gratitude, was, that he would be kind to her mother, and to the friends and servants she left behind her.

Charles Gustavus then conducted her to her apartments, and a few hours afterwards he was crowned in the Cathedral of Upsala.

He had the good taste to show as little display as possible in the ceremony. The Swedish treasury was not in a condition to bear another coronation like the last, and whatever exultation he might have felt, it would have been indecorous to exhibit rejoicings before Christina.

Thus was completed the extraordinary spectacle of a young Queen quitting voluntarily a throne which she had inherited from illustrious ancestors, and which she had made more famous by her own great qualities, and by her sagacious yet mild and tolerant rule.

The two most celebrated examples of a similar act resemble Christina's abdication only in name.

Diocletian and Charles V. were both exhausted in mind and body by anxiety, by the fatigues of continual campaigns, and by satiety of absolute power, before they sought repose, one in watching the growth of his cabbages, the other in listening to the chanting of monks. Christina was only twenty-eight years old when she abdicated, and the jealousy of her nobles had allowed her so much power only as might be expected to whet, rather than to satiate, the ambition of an active and ardent mind. She had no taste for cabbages or monks, and she had no idea of retiring from the world because she quitted the throne.

Her resignation was more unnatural than that of the Roman or of the German Emperor, and she was probably less happy than either of them in her retirement.

Her life did not cease to be serviceable to the

increase and diffusion of science, literature, and taste, still less did it cease to be instructive.

Any one disposed to quit his natural and destined path of duty may well take a lesson from the career of Christina.

Few possess the resources of a mind so richly stored, and fewer still have such means of indulging every refined and elegant taste.*

The world had been ransacked by generals and scholars to complete her library, and to adorn her collections. The possession of these treasures combined with her own fame to preserve the homage of the most intellectual men, and few persons have ever been able to appreciate such means of enjoyment better than Christina ; yet she was restless and dissatisfied from the time that she

* The Chancellor gives instructions :—

'Afven Fältmarskalken påminnas, att, om han får in någre papistiske orter, der sköne och kostelige biblioteker äro till finnandes, såsom förleden sommar i Neiss och Olmutz, böckerna må sändas till Sverige.' — Geijer. 'Svenska Folkets Historia.' Tredje Delen. P. 372.

'Rikskansleren hade noga akt på sådant. Då Gustaf Horn vid Danska krigets utbrott om vintern 1644, inföll Skåne, instruerar Kansleren hans Sekretaire, att påminna Fältmarskalken, att der någre Bibliothecæ publicæ finnas, enkannerligen, der någre Manuscripta äre till fångs, sådant ej må distraheras utan till Stockholm förskickas.' Till Samuel Andersson d. 24 Feb., 1644. Registr. Apud Geijer.

ceased to perform those functions for which she was fitted by her birth and talents.

She endeavourd to persuade the world of her satisfaction by causing a medal to be struck, which represented Mount Olympus, with Pegasus on the summit. The inscription was 'Sedes hæc solio potior.'

There is little doubt that she soon began, and never ceased, to repent of the step she had taken. Far from enjoying the coveted repose, she was more than ever absorbed in politics, when she could no longer interfere in them with dignity.

Her literary meetings lost half their joyousness from the time that they were no longer her relaxation from the duties of government. She must often have thought of the merry conversations, when the greatest scholars of Europe sought a word or a smile from her, and might have applied to herself the Poet's lamentation,

> " Nessun maggior dolore
> Che ricordarsi del tempo felice
> Nella miseria."

After her abdication the difference of opinion which had existed regarding her merits became exaggerated in the highest degree.

The Catholic writers were enthusiastic in her praise; they represented her genius and her excellence as equally unrivalled.

The Protestants depicted her as a monster of depravity. We shall be justified in taking her early character as the basis of our opinion; we shall continue to see industry and energy sometimes misapplied, but we shall find no symptoms of indolence or luxury, or of those ignoble vices which appear incompatible with all that is really known of her character.

167

CHAPTER IV.

Christina's Departure from Sweden—Her Occasional Assumption of Masculine Garb—Meeting with Condé—Journey in State to Brussels—Abjuration of the Lutheran Faith—Various Opinions expressed on this Event—Death of the Queen Dowager, her mother, and of the Chancellor Oxenstiern—Her Relations with her Literary Protegés—Public Profession of the Roman Catholic Faith at Inspruck—Letter to King Charles Gustavus—Reasons for selecting Rome as her Residence—Magnificent Present to the Virgin at Loretto—Public Entry into Rome—Assumes the name of Alessandra on her Confirmation—Magnificent Entertainments in her Honour—Her Indecorous Behaviour at Church—The Pope in Trouble—A Cardinal in Love—Jealousies among her Courtiers—Founds an Academy at Rome—Difficulties from Want of Money—Her Visit to France—Guise's Account of her Appearance and Manners—Received at Fontainebleau by Mademoiselle de Montpensier—Treachery and Death of Monaldeschi—General Disapprobation excited by Christina's Absolute Conduct—Her Reception at Paris—The Count de Nogent's Rebuff—Her Presentation to Louis XIV., by Mazarin—Her Meeting with Henrietta of England—Attends a Meeting of the French Academy—French Appreciation of her Knowledge and Wit—Indiscreet Interference—Visit to Ninon l'Enclos—Cold Reception

on her Second Visit to France—Cromwell gives her no
Encouragement to Visit England—Report of Mazarin's
Intended Intrigue.

CHRISTINA's first feeling after her abdication seems
to have been one of satisfaction at having gained
her own way, but it was a satisfaction not unmixed with regret. When Brahe begged her not
to hurry her departure from Upsala, she replied,
" Would you have me stay here to behold another
in possession of the power which so lately belonged
to me ?"

She only remained five days at Stockholm
before she set out on her travels, but as the people
did not like the idea of her treasures being carried
out of the country, she caused a report to be circulated that she was only about to take the waters
at Spa and then to return. She also concealed
the route which she intended to take. A fleet was
equipped for the purpose of escorting her to
Germany, when she suddenly determined to travel
by land to Denmark.

Baron Lind escorted her to the frontier, and
before he took leave, he delivered a message from
the King, repeating the offer of his hard, but

Christina replied, that if she had been inclined to marry, she would have done so whilst she was queen.

As she passed a small stream which formed the boundary between Sweden and Denmark, she exclaimed, " I am free at last! and out of a country to which I hope I shall never return."

On entering the Danish States, she disguised herself as a man and assumed the name of the Count Dohna. She probably took this step not only to escape inpertinent curiosity, but also to avoid the dangers she might have incurred when travelling with a very slender retinue. She wore a man's wig, and had her own hair cut off. Her valet deplored the loss of her luxuriant and beautiful tresses, but she told him to go on cutting, and asked if he supposed she cared about her hair, when she had just parted with a kingdom.*

The Queen of Denmark received information of the young Count's real quality, and was so curious to see the renowned Christina that she went disguised as a servant maid to an inn at which the

---

* 'Coupe, coupe, Jean! veux-tu que j'ai regret à mes cheveux apres avoir quitté un Royaume.'   Le Pourtrait de la Reine Christine.—Cologne, 1668

travellers put up. The disguised Queens met and
conversed, and it is probable that Christina's
penetration was equal to that of her royal sister;
at all events, either by accident or by design, she
expressed some sentiments about the Danish Court
which where very unpalatable to her visitor.

Christina arrived at Hamburg the 10th of July,
when she immediately resumed her own dress and
name. She, however, scandalized the orthodox by
stopping at the house of a Jewish banker, and the
clergy preached openly against her for this act of
impiety.* The rector, however, who delivered his
discourse in her presence on Sunday, was more
flattering, and took for his text the somewhat
hackneyed subject of the Queen of Sheba.

Christina gave him a gold chain in return, but
the favourable impression which this might have
caused was marred by the circumstance that she
accidentally left in Church a finely gilt book, which
on examination proved to be a Virgil. She
remained three weeks at Hamburg, and on the
30th of July the Landgrave of Hesse gave her a
splendid entertainment. She returned home about
midnight, when she resumed her male attire, and

* Adieux des François á la Suède. P 78.

departed immediately, without taking leave of any one, and accompanied only by Count Steinberg and four attendants. She wore the hat and large boots which were then in fashion, a black wig replaced her own fair hair, a carbine was slung over one shoulder and a sword hung from the other.

Her suite were ordered to start the next day, and to meet her the best way they could at Amsterdam. The reason of this strange proceeding was the dangerous state of the roads since Bremen had taken up arms against the Swedes.

On the 6th of August she arrived at Münster, where she went to see some curiosities contained in the Jesuits' College. A brother of the order recognized her from her likeness to a picture, but he was faithful as his brethren had been in Sweden, and Christina passed unnoticed.

She fell in with her suite at Amesfort, on the 9th of August, but in obedience to the orders they received they did not recognize her, and proceeded to Antwerp instead of Amsterdam.

No one penetrated her disguise except the Jesuit at Münster, although her arrival was expected, and the States had given orders that she should be received everywhere with the greatest honours.

Masculine manners were not altogether new to her, and she now acted the character with such life that on one occasion she pretended to make love to a beautiful girl she met on the road. * She would, however, have found it hard to play her part if she had mixed with the people, and one custom she could never have been reconciled to, which was that the Dutch gentlemen often sat at their dinners from ten to twelve hours.

As soon as she was safe at Antwerp, her disguise was again laid aside, and she received visits from all the authorities.

The Archduke Leopold went to see her, but the great Condé sent a gentleman to bargain about formalities, and he refused to visit her because he was told that he was not entitled to exactly the same ceremony as the Archduke.

At last his curiosity prevailed over his dignity, and he entered her presence in disguise, among a crowd of courtiers. Christina recognized him from his picture; but Condé retired immediately

* Petitot's Coll: Vol. LVIII. P 290.

on being discovered, and refused to return. All or nothing! was his only reply to the invitation sent after him.

Some days afterwards it was arranged that the two self-willed personages should meet as if by accident, but even then they were not pleased with one another.

"Cousin," said the Queen, "who would have believed that, after ten years' desire to see each other, we should meet in this manner?"

Another ex-Queen, whose fall had not been voluntary, was also at Antwerp. The unfortunate Elizabeth of Bohemia, and her daughter, the friend of Descartes, went to the theatre to see Christina, but would not visit her, for fear they should not be received with all the honour which they claimed.

When Christina was on the throne, she had paid little attention to etiquette, and it appears strange, although perhaps not unnatural, that she should have been so punctilious after her abdication.

The reigning Queen of a great country was not likely to receive slights. A wandering Queen, without a crown, might not get all the respect which she claimed, and could certainly afford less to overlook any attack on her dignity.

Christina framed a theory of her own as to her position. She thought, although her power was exercised in a smaller sphere than before, that it was as absolute as ever; she had made it her first condition that she should be free from every kind of control, and responsible to God alone; a degree of independence she would hardly have claimed when on the throne.

She also stipulated for absolute authority over all her dependents, and as they entered voluntarily into this compact, they had not more cause to complain of any violent act than subjects who had never consented to place themselves without appeal in the power of a reigning sovereign.

She had not reflected how much more severely the actions of a Queen would be criticised, when her power might be disputed.

Her journey to Brussels was as magnificent as Cleopatra's progress to Tarsus, although a Dutch canal was certainly less appropriate than the Cydnus for such a display.

The barge which conveyed her was fitted up in the

most sumptuous manner; it carried twelve pieces of cannon, and was covered with gilt.

The vessel's course was delayed by the numerous locks on the canal, at each of which the people assembled in crowds to behold the famous Queen of Sweden.

She reached Brussels in the evening, and was received with great pomp; the city was illuminated, and at the gate she entered beautiful fireworks were exhibited, which represented two angels supporting the name of Christina encircled with laurels.

The day after her arrival at Brussels she abjured the Lutheran faith. A priest named Father Guémés received her confession in the presence of the Archduke and the Counts Montecuculli, Fuensaldagna, and Pimentelle. The ceremony was intended to have been private, and only preparatory to her public profession at Rome, but the Catholics could not resist showing their triumph, and all the artillery of Brussels announced the moment when Christina received absolution.

No action of her life injured Christina's fame more than her conversion. In addition to the general reasons which she had herself given the

Prince of Hesse against changing his religion, she was bound by peculiar ties, as the daughter of the great Protestant champion, Gustavus Adolphus. The Catholics indeed are lavish of their praises; but her memory has been pitilessly assailed by all the Protestant writers, whose great object seems to have been to lessen the triumph of the Catholics, by depreciating their convert. If her chief motive was convenience, because she wished to reside in a Catholic country, it would be difficult to defend her conduct; but we have already seen reason to suppose that this was not the case. Her act was freely discussed at the time, and she herself fell in with a book at Rome, called " The History of the Queen of Sweden's Conversion ;" she wrote on the margin : " He who has written concerning it, knows nothing about it; he who knows, has not written."*

It is certain that she did not seek the extravagant praises of her new friends.

The Jesuits of Louvain proposed to place her, on the list of saints, next to Saint Bridget of Sweden, but Christina said, " I should be much

* Galeazzo Gualdo, ' Historia della sacra Real Maesta di Christina,' &c &c.—Roma, 1656

better pleased with my company if they placed me among the philosophers."

The Swedish theologians visited their indignation upon poor Matthiæ, and said that the Queen's slight attachment to the Lutheran Church was owing to his lukewarm exhortations.

Matthiæ wrote to her and blamed the step she had taken, although he expressed himself with his usual moderation; he ended by urging her to work for his favourite scheme, the union of Christian sects.

He was so persecuted by the Lutherans that he resigned his Bishopric, but Christina never ceased to take a lively interest in his welfare, and at different times sent him considerable sums of money.*

While she was at Brussels, Christina received information of her mother's death, upon which she retired into the country and remained for three weeks in the strictest privacy.

Oxenstiern died about the same time. His last thoughts were about the daughter of his beloved

* She wrote to him, ' Je prends part a votre malheur, Ayez patience, et consolez vous sur l'assurance que je vous donne, que je ne vous abandonnerai jamais, et que vous ne manquerez de rien tant que je vivrai.' Archenholtz, Tome IV., p. 230.

friend. He asked those who stood about his death-bed what news there was of Christina, and as it appeared from the answer that she had not met with the expected happiness, he sighed as he gasped out his last words, " I told her that she would repent, but still she is the daughter of the great Gustavus."*

He had said that he should die working, and this was literally the case, for he was seized with his last illness at a sitting of the Council, and it was with difficulty that he could be removed to his own house.

Christina kept up her intercourse with some of her old friends, among whom Gassendi seems to have been the only one who praised her for renouncing a throne to cultivate science.

Many of them were indignant that she had put it out of her power to continue her liberalities to them. They thought all they had received was due to their merit, and resented as an injustice the act that rendered her incapable of giving more. The French courtiers, who had gained the most, became her bitterest enemies, and verified the saying of their cynical countryman, that gratitude is

* Chanut, Tome III., p. 472.

but the lively anticipation of further benefits.   It is no slight tribute to Christina's character that her enemies were chiefly among the most worthless of those who had been enriched by her bounty, and that the most estimable men still retained their affection for her.   Gassendi's esteem continued; Bochart still took a lively interest in her welfare; and Heinsius was as devoted to her as ever, although he was one of the few who had not profited by her liberality: he was so disinterested as to purchase manuscripts for her from his own funds, the amount of which was never repaid to him, yet he never ceased to speak well of her.

She invited Ménage to Brussels, and told him she had come so far to see him, that he ought to meet her half-way.   Ménage, however, did not think it worth while to comply with her request.

Vossius was received into favour again, and was employed to arrange her library as it arrived from Sweden, and he seized the opportunity of stealing some more of her books.   Bourdelot asked permission to visit her, but received for answer that she did not want a doctor.

Some years afterwards she again corresponded with him, but the tone of her letters does not indicate much friendship or admiration for her old doctor.

After entering into some particulars about her health, from which it appears that she again allowed herself to be frequently bled, she says, " As for your poetry, to tell you the truth, I do not think much of it, but when I recollect that you are eighty years old, I am surprised that you have made yourself so famous in Apollo's craft. The only thing you want now is to play the fiddle, and I dare say you will succeed as well as Socrates did.

" I like mutual compliments, but you poets are as chary of them as Alexander's tutor, who provoked his illustrious pupil to write complaints from the extremity of Asia. Smoke is cheaper in our time."

At Limburg she was visited by Charles II. of England, accompanied by the Duke of Gloucester; and it is unfortunate that no particulars have been preserved of the conversation between the Prince in search of a kingdom, and the Queen who had just resigned one.

Christina's public confession of the Catholic faith took place at Inspruck.

Alexander VII. had just succeeded to the Papal throne, and was not only gratified at Christina's conversion, but was anxious to persuade the world that he was personally the cause of it. He sent Holsteinius as his legate to meet her at Inspruck, and receive her confession. Holsteinius was a convert himself, and a man of learning, as might be expected of the librarian of the Vatican.

He was also a man of the world, and knew how to diversify doctrinal exhortations by accounts of the libraries, galleries, and scholars of Rome. She gratified him in return by her docility, and promised to obey implicitly the Pope's instructions.

Her confession this time was made as public as possible. She entered the Cathedral dressed in plain black silk, with no ornament except a splendid diamond cross. The Archduke led her in, and she was met by a procession of the Clergy.

Holsteinius then read his commission from the Pope to receive her confession. She knelt on a velvet cushion at the foot of the altar, and read the declaration required of her, in a loud and distinct voice.

She began by reciting the Nicene Creed. After that she declared her belief in all the traditions and observances of the Church, and confessed that the Church was the only interpreter of Scripture. She stated her firm belief in seven true and distinct Sacraments, of which Baptism, Confirmation, and Holy Orders might not be received a second time without sacrilege. She accepted the doctrine announced by the Tridentine Synod, concerning original sin and justification. She admitted that the real body and blood of Christ were received in the Eucharist. She declared her belief in Purgatory; she recognized the intercession of saints, acknowledged the propriety of praying to them, of reverencing their relics, of preserving and honouring their images. Finally, she declared that the Church had the power of granting indulgences, and that the exercise of this power was particularly useful to the Christian flock.

No important point of the Roman doctrine was omitted. As the proof and consummation of her orthodoxy, Christina anathematized all those who believed less than herself, and for this pious act she received the absolution of Holsteinius.

In order that there might be no mistake afterwards, she was required to sign four copies of her confession. One of them was deposited in the archives of Inspruck, one was sent to the Vatican, the Pope himself kept one, and the last was given to Christina, that she might not forget what she believed.

After the ceremony was over, a Jesuit preached a sermon on the text, " Hearken, O daughter, and consider, incline thine ear : Forget also thine own people, and thy Father's house."

Whatever emotion Christina may have felt, she showed no signs of it at this pointed address.

She wrote to the new King of Sweden from Inspruck, the 4th of November, 1655 :—

" My Brother,—I have arrived here safely, and have received permission from His Holiness to declare openly what has long been a secret.

" I am happy to obey him, and consider this a greater glory than that of reigning over the powerful states which you possess.

" You ought to be pleased at this step of mine, even if you believe it to be mistaken, since it is so useful and so glorious to you.

" I declare, nevertheless, that the sentiments of friendship which I have always felt for you remain undiminished.

" My love for Sweden is also unchanged; it

will continue so whilst I live, and I shall always remain, your affectionate sister and friend,

"CHRISTINA."*

There were many reasons which led Christina to think of fixing her residence in Italy and at Rome. The fine climate, the libraries, and the works of art were not the only recommendations: Rome had peculiar attractions for an ex-sovereign.

Even Christina was aware that she must, in some degree, submit to the authority of that government to whose protection she trusted. Everywhere but at Rome, she would have found the authority and the protection equally galling. The finest regions of Europe were subject to petty sovereigns—Christina had never considered them as equals; to acknowledge them now as superiors, would have been most humiliating. The case was different at Rome. The proudest knees had bent to the Head of the Church, and the proudest hands had held the stirrup of the Bishop of Rome. Religious humility had often been professed by the most arrogant and ambitious sovereigns. Christina could lose nothing by deference to the Pope: any obedience she might find it necessary to show would

* Galeazzo Gualdo.   P. 110.

be rendered to the Holy Father, and not to the Italian Prince.

The union of the temporal and spiritual authority, which had often proved so embarrassing to those who wielded it, was exactly suited to humour the pride of a royal subject.

Christina accordingly directed her steps to Italy. She was met at Ferrara by a Papal legate, who expressed his surprise at her acquaintance with the finest pictures and the most famous singers at Rome. She spoke of the cathedrals in a way to please her new friends. She said that the three finest in Europe were St. Peter's, the Duomo at Milan, and St. Paul's in London; but added, with a sigh, that the last was now only a stable.

At Bologna she was entertained with fêtes and games. At Ancona there was a representation of the seven hills of Rome, and a river of wine flowed beneath to imitate the Tiber.

She gained the reputation of piety at Loretto by presenting the Virgin with upwards of three hundred and sixty diamonds, and the remainder of her route was marked by fêtes of all kinds, by fireworks, illuminations, and triumphal arches.

On the 19th of December she reached Rome, and according to etiquette she was supposed to enter the city *incognita*, but the concourse of people and the illuminations proved that this was a fiction, and made Christina inquire laughingly whether it was thus that people entered Rome in private.

She was conducted at once into the Pope's presence, and proved her orthodoxy satisfactorily by kissing his foot, but Alexander raised her immediately, and led her to a regal seat covered with gold.

A few days afterwards she made her public entry into Rome through the Porta del Popolo.

The ingenuity of the authorities was taxed to the utmost to make the display as brilliant as possible.

The spectacle was like an old Roman triumph revived. Rich dresses, garlands of flowers, and triumphal arches enlivened the scene; the troops were all under arms, and bands of music were stationed along her route; but the fairest ornaments of all were the Roman ladies in their holiday attire.

Christina's head was so turned by the homage

she had received in Italy that she was persuaded to appear as an Amazon. She rode a white horse in the way that Amazons are supposed to have ridden, but not in the way that European ladies in modern times have considered decorous.

The procession was met at St. Peter's by the dignitaries of the Church, who conducted Christina to the High Altar.

In this fantastic guise she received the rite which most Christians consider the solemn ordinance, and which the Catholics consider the Sacrament, of Confirmation. It was not unusual to take an additional name at this ceremony, and Christina took the name of Alessandra, either in compliment to Alexander VII., or in remembrance of Alexander the Great.

When she was settled in Rome, her time was spent in a manner more consistent with her previous character. She examined with enthusiasm the buildings, monuments, ruins, and works of art, which her knowledge of the history and literature of Rome enabled her thoroughly to appreciate.

Her admiration was not confined to antique productions. She was greatly struck with a statue of Truth by Bernini, who was then at the height of his fame, and she exclaimed several times, "Ah! how beautiful!" "God be praised," said a Cardinal, "that your Majesty loves truth, which personages of your rank seldom care about."

"That is very likely," replied Christina, "for the truth is not always of marble."

Scarcely an evening passed without some fête being given in her honour. The Roman nobles vied with one another in their attentions to the converted Queen. Prince Pamphili gave her an entertainment which cost 40,000 crowns, and Barberini gave one still more splendid.

She visited the College de Propagandâ Fide, and inspected the printing presses, which were working in twenty-two languages. Eight of these stamped the same flattering salutation a few minutes after her arrival: "May Christina live for ever!"

In each of the twenty-two tongues, a scholar addressed some words of homage and flattery to the Queen, which were afterwards printed by the presses under the title of "The Concordance of Languages in the praise of Christina."

The Pope soon made the discovery that his favourite convert might occasionally be troublesome. She did not behave much better at church in Rome than she had done in Sweden, and she used to make the Cardinals as bad as herself, for she often engaged them in conversation while the service was going on.

The Pope himself gave her a hint. He sent her a rosary, and recommended her to use it in prayer time, to prevent her attention from wandering.

Christina knew very well what he meant, and answered that she did not intend to be a Catholic according to the rosary.

There was certainly nothing about rosaries in the confession of faith she had signed, so that she had some reason on her side.

The Pope might have considered himself happy if this had been the only trouble caused him by the young Queen, but among other things she turned the head of one of his Cardinals. Colonna, then fifty years old, fell desperately in love with her.

His age had not taught him discretion, and he took so little pains to conceal his passion that he was ridiculed by every one, and by no one more so than by the lively and satirical Queen.

He was persuaded by some mischievous friend
to powder his head, in order to captivate Christina, but as his venerable appearance did not
produce the desired result, he next began to
perform serenades under her window, and seemed
determined to prove the truth of the old saying,
that "in love affairs there is no fool like an old
fool."

Alexander VII. was a Pope of very different
character from the last of that name. His own
life had always been correct, and he warned the
Cardinal that Christina had not come to Rome
to be scandalized. Colonna did not take the
hint, and the consequence was that he was sent
out of Rome.

Christina began to find that trivial matters
disturbed her leisure, and interfered with her
peace as much as affairs of state had done.
Her Spanish courtiers were enraged because she
took some Italians into her service.

Pimentelle and Cueva allied themselves with
the Cardinals of the Spanish party, and a plot of
some sort was formed against Christina. She
consequently dismissed Cueva in a very harsh
manner, and warned him that if he ever spoke

disrespectfully of her, she would reach him, wherever he might be.

She told the Cardinal de' Medici, who was attached to the Spanish party, that if Cueva had not been a General in the service, she would have dismissed him in a still more ignominious way.

Even Pimentelle, who had stood so high in her favour, did not fare much better, and her enemies did not fail to dilate on her violence and capriciousness.

It appears, however, from a writer who was not very partial to Christina, that Cueva was both whimsical and impertinent.

He refused to pass through one of her apartments, because it contained a portrait of Louis XIV. When Christina discovered this, she shut up the room which he passed through to avoid the picture; but Cueva was not to be shamed out of his childishness, and displayed his ill-humour more and more.*

The Queen's time, however, was not monopolized by these paltry squabbles.

She founded an academy to which all the most eminent Italians in Rome belonged. The meet-

* Petitot's Coll. Tome LVIII.

ings were held once a week in her apartments, and she used to preside. The subjects most frequently discussed were poetry, philology, and antiquities, and the meeting generally finished with music.

These occupations were not sufficient to satisfy her mind.

The amusements of Italy were exhausted, and Christina felt for them the same satiety that she had experienced for the Swedish banquets and revels :—

> "Quid terras alio calentes
> Sole mutamus patria ?   Quis exul
> Se quoque fugit ?"

The Roman fêtes were monotonous, and she wished to see the more lively proceedings of the French Court.

An epidemic disease was her pretext for leaving Rome, but her revenues were so much in arrear, in consequence of the Polish War into which Charles Gustavus had plunged, that she found it difficult to raise funds for the journey. She was obliged to sell her carriages and horses, to pawn her jewels, and to accept a contribution of 20,000 crowns from the Pope.

She arrived at Marseilles the 24th July, 1656. The French Government consulted precedents as to the forms with which she should be received, and it happened that the one which was chosen as a guide was the reception of the Emperor Charles V.

The Duke of Guise was sent to meet her. His life had been as romantic as that of Christina, and he was compared to one of the ancient Paladins of France.

At a pageant in Paris, he and Condé had each led a troop of cavaliers, and they were called the Hero of History and the Hero of Romance. Guise had lately returned from his unfortunate expedition to Naples, which the scoffing Parisians called the voyage of the Argonauts, and his ill success had not left him in the humour to relish his occupation of escorting the Queen. He wrote an account of her to one of his friends, by whom it was read to Louis XIV.

"As I am exceedingly dull here, I will try and divert you by giving an account of the Queen whom I am accompanying.

" She is not tall, but well-made; her arm is

handsome, her hand white and well-formed, but more like a man's than a woman's. One shoulder is rather higher than the other, but she conceals the defect so well with her strange dress and movements, that one might make a bet about it. Her face is large, and all her features are strongly marked; her nose is aquiline, her mouth large, but not unpleasant, and her teeth are pretty good.

" Her eyes are beautiful, and full of animation. Her complexion is good, but she has an extraordinary head-dress. This is a man's wig, made very large and high in the front. She wears a great deal of powder, and seldom any gloves; she uses men's boots, and has the voice and manners of a man. She is very polite; speaks eight languages well, and particularly French, as if she had been born in Paris. She knows more than all our Academy and the Sorbonne put together; she is an admirable judge of paintings, and of everything else. She knows more of the intrigues of our Court than I do myself—in fact, she is an extraordinary person.

" I am accompanying her to Paris, so that you will be able to judge for yourself. I do not think I have omitted anything from her portrait, except that she sometimes wears a sword and a buff jerkin."*

Christina was treated with profound respect in all the towns she passed through. The keys were presented to her, and brilliant fêtes celebrated her arrival.

At ·one place a priest greeted her with the words: "Sweden made you Christina; Rome made you Christian; may France make you Most Christian."†

This indicated a wish, of course, that she might marry Louis XIV.; and Chanut said that she would willingly have consented to this alliance; but it does not appear that she ever had the offer.

Christina passed through Avignon, Lyons, Auxerre, and Sens, and was received at Fontaine-bleau by the celebrated Mademoiselle de Mont-pensier.

She was not pleased with the familiarity of the French ladies, and said, "What has possessed them with such a passion for kissing me? Is it because I am like a man?"

---

* Madame de Motteville.—Petitot's Coll., Tome XXXIX., p. 376. Paris, 1824.

† 'Fecit te Suecia Christinam; Roma Christianam; faciat te Gallia Christianissimam.'—Fryxell, Kap. XXIX.

On the other hand, Mademoiselle, though occasionally somewhat masculine herself, was shocked at Christina's behaviour.

The two royal ladies went to the theatre together, and we may imagine the horror of Mademoiselle when her companion exclaimed aloud, swore, stretched her legs over the back of her chair, lay down, and put herself in various strange postures.

On a subsequent occasion, Mademoiselle went o see her late in the day. She found her friend in bed, with a napkin tied round her head instead of a nightcap. Here and there her bare head appeared through the covering, for Christina had just been shaved, and we may easily believe the French lady, that the costume was very unbecoming.

Two hundred thousand persons filled the streets to witness Christina's arrival in Paris, besides those who occupied every window along her route. The Provost of the merchants met her outside the gates, and, kneeling at her feet, presented her with the keys. She attended the service at Notre Dame, and then went to the apartments provided for her at the Louvre.

In the polished capital of France, Christina did not make any alteration in her manners, and the Court wits were inclined to make merry at her expense; but, with all her eccentricity, she had so much dignity that a look from her generally over-awed them.

The Count de Nogent hazarded some jokes about her, which were repeated again. He often made himself ridiculous by his long stories. He began to give some dull particulars, in her presence, about a siege of Valenciennes a hundred years before. Christina stopped him abruptly, and begged him to postpone his story for another hundred years. The company were highly amused at this rebuff, and Nogent did not risk any more encounters with the Queen.

After a few days' residence in Paris, Christina went to see the Queen Dowager and the young King at Compiègne.

She stopped the first day at Chantilly, where Mazarin met her, and introduced Louis XIV. es "a distinguished young gentleman." Christina immediately replied, " I believe it well, for he seems born to wear the crown." Mazarin said that it was difficult to deceive her, and acknowledged the rank of her visitor. The young King was, at this time, very shy; but she soon managed to engage him in conversation, and to set him at ease.

The next day she went to Compiègne, and was met three leagues from that place by the King and his mother in state.

Christina alighted from her carriage as soon as she saw Anne of Austria.

The French Queen did the same, and they advanced to meet one another.

Louis gave Christina his hand, and she took precedence of Anne, which appeared not to have been his intention, as he afterwards reproached his mother for forgetting her dignity.

Christina knew that the Queen Dowager loved flattery even better than precedence, and accidentally discovered that she was very proud of her white hands and arms.

She took an early opportunity of asking leave to examine a bracelet which contained a portrait of the young King.

Anne of Austria took off her glove and raised her arm. Christina said no more about the brace-let or the portrait, but began at once to admire the hand and arm. The flattery was so evidently acceptable that she went on to say she would have been repaid for her journey from Rome if it had brought no other advantage than the sight of the most beautiful hand and arm in the world.

Christina attended the administration of the Sacrament at Notre Dame during her residence in Paris, but it was said she talked all the time to some of the Bishops; and if so they were more blamable than she was. She confessed to the Bishop of Amiens, and he said that she did so with great devotion, and that he was more edified by her sentiments than by her manners.*

Poor Henrietta of England paid her a visit, and the abdicated Queen had some cause for reflection when she heard that her royal sister was reduced to such poverty that she was obliged sometimes to remain in bed to save firing.

Christina attended a meeting of the French Academy, which does not appear to have been very brilliant.

The Chancellor expressed his regret that no particular subject had been prepared for her amusement. He said that in the ordinary course a

* Petitot's Coll. Vol. XLII. P. 87.

lecture would be delivered on " Grief," which would be appropriate to the occasion in so far as it might express their grief at her approaching departure.

A sheet of the celebrated Dictionary of the Academy, which was then in progress, was next read.

It happened that the word " Jeu" was the subject.

In the article the expression occurs, " Ce sont jeux de Princes, qui ne plaisent qu'à ceux qui les font."*

The subject was not happily chosen.

Christina thought at first that an affront was intended to her, and she coloured deeply; but when she felt that the eyes of all present were upon her, she soon recovered herself, and pretended to laugh, although it was easy to see that her merriment was forced.

Notwithstanding her eccentricity, the Parisians appreciated her wit and her talent for repartee: her intimate acquaintance with everything remarkable in the country was certainly a compliment to the people she visited.

On one occasion she told the Marquis de Sourdis

* Memoires de Conrant: Petitot's Coll. Vol. XLVIII. P. 181.—Dictionnaire de L'Académie Françoise. Art. Jeu.

more than he knew himself about his own picture gallery. Another time she maintained, in opposition to several French people who ought to have been well informed, that there was an agate of extraordinary beauty in a chapel at St. Denis, and an expedition to the place proved the truth of her assertion.

Although the refined ladies of the French Court ridiculed her manners, yet one of the least friendly among them admitted that there was no stain on her character, and remarked, very justly, that if there had been anything against her, it would certainly have been published by the charitable people about the Court.*

The men, however, as usual, admired her more than the women did.

Patru, who was considered unrivalled in his knowledge of the French language, and who was chiefly famous for his severe and caustic criticisms, addressed her as follows :—

"Your Majesty in early youth, and surrounded by everything which could soften and corrupt the mind, resisted all these temptations and applied yourself to the study of wisdom.

* Madame de Motteville.

"The knowledge of language, in the pursuit of which we spend days and nights, and to which we devote all the best years of our lives, was the amusement of your Majesty's childhood.

"Literature offers no flowers or fruits which have not been gathered by your hands. Your genius has explored the whole circle of the sciences. You have done what few men have accomplished, and what no other woman has even dared to attempt; and all this, Madam, although surrounded by the pomps of royalty and the hindrances of a court."

She went to a theatrical performance in which the actors were Jesuits, and which she did not hesitate to criticize severely: shortly afterwards, when Father Arnauld waited upon her to hear some complaints she had to make about the Jesuits in Rome, she told him that she accepted his excuses, as she did not wish to have the order for her enemies, but that she would never choose one of them for a confessor, or an actor.

A performance by professional actors did not please her much better. Some one who was anxious to excuse the taste of the French Court, told the Queen that the actors generally performed better. " I suppose so," was the dry reply, " or you would not keep them."

Before Christina left France she effaced all the favourable impressions caused by her flattery of the Queen Dowager.

Louis XIV. was so violently in love with Mademoiselle Mancini, a niece of Cardinal Mazarius, that for some time he seriously intended to marry her. Anne of Austria, and even the Cardinal himself, opposed so unsuitable a match; but for some reason or other Christina professed unusual sympathy for the lovers, and told the young King, "If I were in your place, nothing in the world should hinder me from marrying the woman I loved."

After this indiscreet interference, Annie of Austria was naturally anxious to get rid of her guest.

Christina left Compiègne for Italy on the 23rd of September, 1656. She stopped at Senlis, to visit Ninon l'Enclos, so famous for her beauty, her talents, and her faults. Christina was not insensible to the fascinations of this remarkable woman, whose name has become as widely known as that of Aspasia, and who was not thought unworthy of the friendship of Madame de Maintenon and of many ladies of good . character.

Some enemies of Christina have said that Ninon l'Enclos was the only lady for whom she expressed any strong feelings of admiration. Her letter to Ebba Sparre, written shortly after her interview with Ninon, will be the best answer to this accusation, and will prove that Christina was capable of a strong and lasting affection for one of her own sex.

"Pesaro, March, 1657.

. . . . "In whatever part of the world I may be, I shall never cease to think of you. The person who brings you this letter can witness how often I speak of your goodness and beauty.

. . . . "Can I be consoled when condemned to an eternal separation from you? If I may never see you again I shall always love you, and you would be very cruel to doubt it.

"A friendship proved by three years' absence cannot be suspected. It is impossible for you to lose my friendship; while I live I will not cease to love you. I should be the happiest princess in the world if I could have you as the witness of my happiness, and if I could have the satisfaction of being useful to you. If an opportunity offers be assured that possibility will be the only limit to

my services. Adieu, be happy, and remember me,—   " CHRISTINA ALESSANDRA.

" Give my compliments to all my friends, and assure them that if I have not the same tenderness for
them as for you, I have at least the same constancy."

Christina returned to Rome by way of Turin,
where she was hospitably received by the Duke o
Savoy. Rome appeared dull after Paris, and she
very soon made arrangements for returning to the
French capital. The excuse she made did not
seem to indicate a very high opinion of Louis the
Fourteenth's sense, for she said she only wished to
be at Paris to see the young King dance at a grand
ballet. The French Court had been willing to fête
her on her first visit, but they had no idea of
encouraging Christina to establish herself in Paris

When she arrived in France, a message was sent
to request she would remain either at Lyons or
at Avignon, as they were not prepared for so dis
tinguished a guest in Paris.

As Christina did not take the first hint, but
continued her journey towards the capital, another
message was sent, which assigned the palace of
Fontainebleau as her residence.

Here she waited impatiently for an invitation to Paris. Week after week passed away without the invitation, and she could no longer doubt that she was an unwelcome guest.

Whilst she was in this irritable mood, the tragedy was performed with which Christina's name is inseparably connected.

The execution of Monaldeschi in the French King's palace was a violent and unjustifiable act, but without excusing it, we may certainly argue that it was not a crime of such enormity as has been commonly represented. The darkest accusation, that Monaldeschi had been Christina's favoured lover, is totally without foundation.

There is every reason to believe that Christina never had a guilty attachment for him or for any one else. A mystery hangs over the whole affair, but it is most probable that the execution of Monaldeschi was the punishment for political, and not for personal offences; and that, notwithstanding its irregularity, it should rather be considered as an execution than as a murder.

Very soon after Christina resigned her own throne, she entered into intrigues to gain another, and all through her career political schemes give the clue to her preference for individuals. Even her favour to Magnus de la Gardie was caused, in some degree, by her wish to balance the power of the Oxenstierns.

Chaunt, Uhlfeld, Bourdelot, Pimentelle and others, were caressed or disgraced from political motives.*

When she first left Sweden she had expectations from Spain. She wished to use the Spanish interest with Rome, and she had some idea of getting the Government of the Netherlands.

The French and Spaniards were such bitter enemies, that there was no possibility of favouring one party without slighting the other. Christina

* Evelyn says that he was acquainted with a Signor Pietro, a famous musician who had been long at Christina's Court.

'He spake high things of that romantic Queen's learning, and skill in languages, the majesty of her behaviour, her exceeding wit, and that the histories she had read of other countries, especially of Greece and Rome, had made her despise her own. That the real reason of her resigning the Crown was the noblemen importuning her to marry, and the promise which the Pope had made her of procuring her to be Queen of Naples, which also caused her to change her religion; but she was cheated by his crafty Holiness working on her ambition. That the reason of her killing her Secretary at Fontainebleau was his revealing that intrigue with the Pope.' Evelyn's Diary. Vol. II., p. 149.

favoured Pimentelle and the Spanish party, until she became convinced that there was nothing to be gained in that quarter : she then, as already related, disgraced the Spaniards and returned to the French, in anticipation of her proposed visit to Paris.

By this policy she ultimately made both French and Spaniards her enemies ; but it must be admitted, to her credit, that so far from fomenting the hostility of the two great Catholic powers, she constantly tried to reconcile them.

Her Italian favourites were chosen for the purpose of strengthening her interest in Rome, and the Marquis Monaldeschi was the most contemptible of these favourites.

Writers the most unfriendly to Christina describe him as greedy, selfish, and ungrateful, false and dishonourable.*

He was a bitter enemy of another Italian in her service, named Sentinelli, and in the depth of his malice he formed a plan to injure Christina and

* ' Johan, Markis de Monaldeschi, var född i Rom och of förnäm slägt. Alla författare beskrifva honom såsom egenkär, påflugen, otacksam, squalleraktig samt utan heder och pålitighet.' And. Fryxell, ' Berättelser ur Svenska Historien.' 10 Delen. P. 254.

Sentinelli at the same time, by divulging her secrets, and by making her believe that Sentinelli was the traitor.

He imitated Sentinelli's style and forged his hand-writing, and took measures to let the letters fall into Christina's hands. The exact tenor of them does not appear, but a contemporary writer says that they were both injurious and insulting to the Queen, although their subject had nothing to do with love.*

Christina soon began to suspect the real culprit. Some letters addressed to him were intercepted by her orders, and they left no doubt of his guilt.

Whilst these proofs of his treachery were collecting, she pretended to place her usual confidence in Monaldeschi.

One day, in conversation with him, she turned the subject to the calumnies which were circulated about her. He replied, " These stories must proceed from some one intimately acquainted with your Majesty's affairs; it would seem they must be written either by Sentinelli or by myself: Your Majesty will soon discover the traitor, and I entreat you not to spare him."

† Courtin. Apud Fryxell. P. 255.

Christina asked, "What punishment does such treachery deserve?"

Monaldeschi, who thought that he was pronouncing sentence upon his rival, said :—

"Your Majesty ought to execute him without pity ; such a punishment would be so just that I should beg to be allowed to perform it with my own hand."

"Very well," replied the Queen, "recollect what you have said, and be assured that I will not spare the traitor."

In the meantime letters fell into her hands which were in Monaldeschi's own hand-writing, signed by himself, and which left no doubt of his guilt.

Christina sealed them up in a packet, and placed them in the care of Father Le Bel, the Prior of the convent. She then related the whole story to one of the monks, only suppressing the names, and asked him what such a traitor deserved.

The monk answered that he deserved to die.

Monaldeschi began to perceive that something was wrong. He could not understand why he did not get the letters which he expected.

Other things increased his distrust so much that he destroyed a number of his papers, and wore a light cuirass under his clothes.

Such artifices were too shallow to deceive Christina's penetration, and such a defence was too feeble to resist her vengeance. In spite of his efforts, his pale and downcast countenance betrayed his disquietude, and when too late he made some preparations for flight.

On the first of November, Christina sent for him to the Gallery of the Stags, so named from the hunting trophies of the French kings which decorated the walls. This was the place she selected to strike her quarry.

She received him as usual, and began to talk about indifferent subjects, but a few minutes afterwards Sentinelli entered, accompanied by two soldiers, at the same time that Father Le Bel approached from the other side. Christina ordered them all to come near, and then asked Le Bel for the packet of letters with which he had been entrusted.

She broke the seal, and first of all taking the forged letters, asked Monaldeschi if he knew any-. thing about them. He pleaded ignorance, upon which Christina produced other letters in his own undisguised writing.

Even then the wretched man endeavoured to throw the guilt on others, but at last he fell on his knees and begged for mercy.

Sentinelli and the soldiers now drew their swords; but Monaldeschi prayed for some delay, and for a hearing.

Christina gave him both. She walked up and down the gallery in conversation with him for an hour.

At the end of that time she demanded some papers which he had on his person. They were examined, and proved to be in his own hand-writing, and of the same tenor as the others.

This last proof was decisive, and Monaldeschi no longer attempted to excuse himself.

Christina turned to Le Bel and said—"My Father, I leave this man in your hands, prepare him for death, and take care of his soul!"

Monaldeschi fell at her feet and prayed for mercy. He confessed that he had in that very room advised her to execute the traitor, and he acknowledged that he himself was the traitor; but he begged that his life might be spared, and his punishment commuted to banishment from Europe.

Christina told him that it was better to die than to live disgraced, and so saying she turned from him and left the room.

The soldiers now ordered Monaldeschi to make haste and confess himself. He knelt to Le Bel, but not to confess. He entreated the priest to intercede for him with Christina, and his prayers were so urgent that Le Bel consented to make the attempt. He kept his promise, and begged with tears for Monaldeschi's pardon. He reminded the Queen that she was not in her own palace, and that the French King might not be pleased at such summary justice.

Christina replied, " I am neither an exile nor a prisoner ; I have the right to punish my servants, and am only answerable to God for my actions."

The good Father then tried another argument. He reminded her of her reputation for mildness and wisdom; this reputation would be placed in jeopardy by an action which many people would think violent and hasty; and he added that if she proceeded against the culprit according to law, his punishment would then bring no odium upon her.

"What!" said Christina, "shall I, who have absolute authority over my followers, go to law with one of them, when I have full proofs of his treason under his own hand?"

"Still," pleaded Le Bel, "your Majesty is a party in this affair, and ought not at the same time to be a judge."

"My father," said Christina, "my conscience does not allow me to comply with your request; go therefore and prepare the wretch for death."

The good Prior was much concerned at being obliged to take a part in this tragedy, and returned with tears in his eyes to tell Monaldeschi that he must die.

The unfortunate man now showed as much want of courage and manliness as he had previously shown want of faith and honour.

He knelt down twice and began his confession, and as many times he rose to cry and supplicate for mercy.

He had pronounced his own doom when he thought he was sealing the death-warrant of Sentinelli, but the latter felt a degree of pity which he would not have experienced from his rival. Sentinelli consented to make an appeal

himself to the Queen, but a display of pusillani-
mity was not the way to move Christina. When
she heard that Monaldeschi would not finish his
confession, and sought thus to prolong his life, she
exclaimed :—

"The coward ! wound him, and thus force him
to confess !"

The precautions the wretched man had taken
to preserve his life, now served only to increase his
misery. Sentinelli tried in vain to wound him
through his shirt of mail, and at last struck him
in the face.

Convinced now that he could not escape death,
Monaldeschi finished his confession and resigned
himself to his fate, but a considerable time elapsed
before the soldiers could complete their bloody
task, on account of the shirt of mail.

There will be hardly any difference of opinion
now that this act of Christina's, even if it be not
called a murder, was a violent and illegal execution. Some impartial writers, however, have
attempted her justification, and amongst them
the illustrious Leibnitz, who at least deserves a
hearing, because he had paid particular attention
to the subject, as is proved by his "Traité sur
le droit de Souveraineté et d'Ambassade."

Leibnitz maintained that, as the suite of a Sovereign or his Minister were exempt from the jurisdiction of the tribunals in countries they visited, the suite must still be accountable to some one for their actions, and could only be so to their own Sovereign or Minister.

A parallel case happened nearly about the same time, which has hardly been considered a matter of reproach to the perpetrator.

When Charles II. was in exile, and it did not appear likely he would ever be King of England, one of his suite, named Manning, was detected corresponding with Thurloe, and he was shot by order of Charles in the palace of the Duke of Neuburg.

Charles passed scathless from the censure which has so deeply wounded the fame of Christina, but he had an advantage not to be desired for her.

Charles committed so many crimes, that we all feel it would be absurd to make a great outcry about one. The only crime which Christina committed was so at variance with her usual placable and indulgent temper, that it stands out in the strongest and most painful relief, and has enabled her enemies to draw her picture as a monster of cruelty.

Christina herself boldly maintained her right to pronounce sentence of death; and there is every reason to believe she was perfectly sincere in her opinion. It must be remembered that not only her servants, but the people of those parts which formed her appanage, took an oath of fidelity to her, and that she named and displaced 'governors, judges, and other officers. Foreign powers also recognized her independence by receiving her ambassadors, and by accrediting noblemen of the highest rank in the same capacity to her.

It would, therefore, be difficult to draw any difference between her rights and those of a reigning prince, and the matter must rather be judged on its own merits than on her want of authority.

Louis XIV. was highly indignant, not so much at the violence of the proceedings, as that any one should so far encroach on his prerogative as to slaughter an inmate of one of his palaces.

Christina was treated with great coldness by the French Court, yet she did not take the hint to hasten her departure.

She was recommended to disavow any partici-

patiou in Monaldeschi's death, and to let it appear
to be the result of a quarrel, but she would not
for a moment throw the responsibility on others.

It was a matter of no little difficulty for the
French Court to get rid of their guest, for she
managed to establish herself again in Paris.

She no longer pleaded her desire to see the
young King dance : she was now anxious to derive
spiritual benefit from the discourses of Père Le
Bouts, the Court preacher, and it would have been
hard to thwart her pious wishes.*

Anne of Austria was heartily tired of her visitor,
and she is reported to have said, that if the Queen
of Sweden would not quit Paris, she should do so
herself.†

Among the means employed to disgust her with
Paris, a plan was made to turn her dancing into
ridicule, but it was not so easy to entrap her. The

---

* ' On ne sauroit chasser d'ici la reine de Suède : elle admire Paris et toutes les raretés de la ville : mais elle a dit
au roi qu'elle a bien envie de profiter tout ce carême prochain
des sermons du père le Bouts. De Paris ce 22 Mars, 1658.'—
' Lettres de ,Guy Patin.'   Paris, 1846.

† Elle s'est partie malcontente de la Reine, ayant appris
qu'elle avoit dit que si la Reine de Suède ne s'en alloit, elle
sortiroit du Louvre.'—Lettres de Guy Patin, p. 383.

party was all arranged, and Christina was present, but could not be persuaded to dance.

The matter had become serious, for Christine had been heard to say that she should quit France with more reluctance than she had done her native land.

It required all Mazarin's skill in diplomacy to ensure her departure, and it was said that among other arguments, he gave her 200,000 livres to return to Rome.

Before she set out, she sent a messenger to Cromwell, who expressed her admiration of his great qualities, and hinted at her desire to see so remarkable a man.

The Protector had no inclination to be placed in any embarrassing position by her freaks. He answered her message accordingly, with polite expressions, but avoided giving her any invitation to England, to the great relief of his wife, who was very jealous of Christina.

It was supposed that Mazarin intended to have carried on an intrigue by her means, the object of which was to persuade the Protector to repudiate his wife, and to marry a niece of the Cardinal's;

but from what Christina already knew of Cromwell, it is not likely she would have taken part in so extravagant a scheme.

CHAPTER V.

Affairs of Sweden after Christina's Abdication — Charles Gustavus's Disposition for War—Invasion of Poland in 1655 —Alliance with Frederick William, Elector of Brandenburg —Abdication of John Casimir—Campaign in Denmark— Charles Gustavus and the Rector of Nyköping—Ambitious Projects of the Swedish Monarch—Treaty of Roskild— Perfidious Aggression on Denmark—Unsuccessful Attack on Copenhagen—Victory of the Dutch over the Swedes in a Naval Engagement—Charles Gustavus's Rejection of the Mediation of England, France, and Holland—Total Defeat of the Swedish Army in Fyen—Death of Charles Gustavus — Christina a Pensionary of Rome — Cardinal Azzolini appointed to Manage her Affairs—Begins the Study of Chemistry—Disputes between Christina and the Pope — Letter written on receiving News of Charles Gustavus's Death—Alarm caused by Christina's Proposed Visit to Sweden—Opposition to the Appointment of Duke Adolphus as Regent — Conduct of Count Brahe and Magnus de la Gardie on the Appearance of Christina in Sweden—Her Memorial to the Diet for the Settlement of her Revenues—Animosity of the Lutheran Clergy—Asser-tion of her Claim, under certain circumstances, to the Throne—Her Compulsory Signature of a Second Act of Renunciation—Letter to the Governor of her Domains—

Residence in Hamburg—Study of Alchemy with the Italian Borri—Her Protegé Lambecius—Return of Christina to Rome—Her Apprehension of Danger to Europe from the Fanaticism and Military Power of the Turks—The French Embassy at Rome — Christina again returns to Sweden — Harsh and Uncourteous Behaviour of the Regents and Council—Manifestations of Popular Sympathy—Her Imprudent Conduct at Hamburg on the Election of Clement IX. as Pope—Rosenback sent as her Envoy to the States—The Counsels of Algernon Sidney and Azzolini in Reference to her Visit to Sweden—The Hostile Decisions of the Council overruled by the States—Christina's Return to Rome—Negotiations for the Polish Throne—Influence on Public Taste exercised by the Academy founded by the Swedish Queen at Rome—Her Intercourse with Literary and Scientific Men—The Swedish Aristocracy—Education of Charles XI.—Aggressive Policy of the Swedish Government—The Triple Alliance—Disgraceful Negotiations of the Swedish Senate—Aggression on Brandenburg—Defeat of the Swedes by the Elector Frederick William—Disgrace and Death of Magnus de la Gardie—Humiliation of the Swedish Nobility—Count Wasenau—Christina's Hatred to Religious Persecution.

It is necessary to take a slight view of the most important events which happened in Sweden, after Christina's abdication, not only in consequence of their direct influence upon her, but also because the benefits of her peaceful policy will be better appreciated, when we see the ruin which an unrestrained passion for war afterwards brought upon Sweden. Three Kings succeeded her, each of whom possessed great military genius, but their incessant wars impoverished their country, lost the fairest portion of their territory, and reduced Sweden to the condition of a third-rate power.

The Swedes gained in Charles Gustavus what they desired, a genuine Protestant, and a King devoted to war.

The orthodox edition of the Bible always lay on his table, prayers were said morning and evening in his household by a Lutheran divine, and he joined in them himself with a loud voice.

His reign of five years was one incessant campaign, and he is reported to have said that a great Prince should be always at war, that he might occupy his subjects, and that he might be feared by his neighbours.*

Soon after Christina's departure, a Council was held at Stockholm, in which it was debated whether Russia, Poland, or Denmark should be the first enemy. The implacable Uhlfeld used all his influence against Denmark, but the Polish renegade Radziejowski again thwarted him, and succeeded in turning the Swedish arms against his own country.

* Memoires du Chevalier de Terlon. Tome I. P. 267.

The pretext used against John Casimir was that, after Christina's abdication, he had again asserted the claims of the elder branch of the Vasa family to the Swedish throne.

These claims had never been abandoned; but John Casimir merely wished that the rights of his family should not lapse for want of a protest.

So far from intending to take any active measures to gain another crown, he was only anxious to be relieved from the weight of the one he already wore.

On the death of his brother Uladislaus, he had been elected King of Poland, and, unfortunately for himself, he married his brother's widow as well as succeeded to his brother's throne. Mary of Gonzaga's restless and ambitious temper soon made the poor King pine for the quiet life he had led as a Jesuit and a Cardinal. The Queen would not allow him to resign his crown, and he was forced into unfortunate wars with Russia and Sweden, and into still more unfortunate quarrels with his own disorderly subjects.

In one of their tumultuous Diets, he gave them the following remarkable warning:—

" Your internal strife and dissensions will invite

your neighbours into fresh wars, and leave your country an easy prey to the enemy. The day will come when Russia will take Lithuania, Brandenburg will take Prussia, and Austria will take the country round Crakau. God grant my prophecy may not be fulfilled!"*

In this prophecy, which has been so literally accomplished, John Casimir did not even mention Sweden, although, at that time, she appeared a much more formidable enemy than Russia, Brandenburg, or Austria; but the thoughtful King based his opinion on general principles, and not on the accidental successes of armies. Charles X. and Charles XII. both overran Poland, but they exhausted Sweden in useless wars, and Russia, Prussia, and Austria reaped the advantages of their brilliant campaigns.

Charles Gustavus invaded Poland in the summer of 1655, and in one campaign reduced the whole country to submission. He then turned against the Elector of Brandenburg, who had raised an army of 28,000 men to support the cause of John Casimir. The Elector was defeated, obliged to

* Fryxell. P. 18.

swear allegiance, and to furnish a contingent to the Swedish army.

During this diversion, however, the Poles recovered from their first stupor, and struggled to throw off the yoke which had been so quickly imposed upon them.

Charles Gustavus returned and defeated the Poles in a desperate battle under the walls of Warsaw, which lasted for three days. The victory was not so complete as it might have been, because Charles' new ally, the Elector of Brandenburg, refused to follow up the enemy.

Frederick William of Brandenburg conducted his affairs with judgment and good fortune. He now made a treaty on more equal terms with Sweden, by which the independence of Prussia was settled, on condition that it should revert to Sweden, if male heirs should fail in the house of Brandenburg.

Soon after the battle of Warsaw, he entered into negotiations with Poland, Austria, and Denmark, for the purpose of restraining the insatiable ambition of the Swedish King.

Although not a very staunch ally, he was the only ally that Charles Gustavus ever had, and this fact may help us to form a just opinion of the latter.*

A few years after these misfortunes, John Casimir lost his beautiful and troublesome wife. Some of his friends, among whom was Louis XIV., urged him to marry again. He replied, " If the King of France wishes me to marry again, he must restore to me some of the years which have vanished."

He now resolved in good earnest to abdicate. He was, for once, inflexible to tears and entreaties, and the Diet passed a resolution that it should, in future, be unlawful for a King of Poland to abdicate.

They never paid him a farthing of the small pension which he requested, but Louis XIV. gave him the rich Abbey of St. Germain, where he ended his career in peace.

The Danes were well aware how nearly the storm had burst on their country instead of on Poland. They knew that Charles would probably attack them next, and they determined to choose their own time for the struggle which appeared inevitable.

* ' Det finnes,' sade Konungen self, ' ingen, som vill spänna sin häst tillsammns med oss.'—Rådsprot, d. 17 Jan. 1660.

They declared war, and hoped to intercept Charles on his return through Dantzic. They learned to their consternation that the whole Swedish army, with the King at its head, was hastening by forced marches through Pomerania and Mecklenburg to Denmark.

The remarkable campaign which ensued is well worthy of consideration. Its general results, however, and not its details, have reference to Christina.

It is sufficient to say that Charles Gustavus took advantage of a severe winter to cross the Little Belt, and, emboldened by his success, performed the more hazardous feat of crossing the Great Belt on the ice.

The Danes were able to make but little resistance, and one place after another fell into the hands of the Swedes.

One of the last towns taken was Nyköping, and as it was unable to pay the contribution demanded, the fierce conqueror announced his intention of burning it to the ground.

It was Sunday, and some of the Swedes attended the service in the parish church. The worthy rector was roused at the sight. He preached eloquently and indignantly on the cruelty of men to one another, to brothers and fellow-Christians.

Charles Gustavus himself was one of the congregation, and the clergyman had hardly reached home when he received a message to say that the King was coming to dine with him. He endeavoured to escape the honour, and said that the Swedish soldiers had robbed him of everything except some peas and bacon.

The King, however, came to dinner, and his host behaved with so much good sense, that the town was spared.

Fortunately for the Danes they did not depend entirely on the moderation of Charles Gustavus. He contemplated uniting Denmark and Norway to the Swedish crown, and was only induced to pause in his career of conquest by the intervention of England, France, and Holland.

Charles Gustavus offered Cromwell a considerable part of Denmark as the price of his co-operation, but the great Protector was not inclined to adopt the royal system of trafficking in the allegiance of people against their wishes. Meadows, the English envoy, protested against the incorpora-

tion of Norway with Sweden, and intimated
plainly that England would not suffer both the
coasts on which she depended for timber and iron
to be in the hands of the same power.

With all his rashness, Charles Gustavus did not
wish to add Cromwell to the number of his enemies,
and although the terms which he exacted at the
peace of Roskild were sufficiently hard upon Denmark, they did not amount to the forfeiture of her
independence.

Charles Gustavus was in no good humour at
having his prey snatched from his grasp.

Count Tot returned with a reconnoitring party
which he had led under the walls of Copenhagen,
just as the King had discovered the necessity of
suspending hostilities.

The Count reported the weakness of the defences;
but the King said that he had changed his plans,
that he should make further acquisitions in
Denmark by diplomacy, and not by the sword,
and that Sten Bjielke and Uhlfeld would attend
to his interests.

"I beg your Majesty's pardon," said the high-
spirited nobleman, "but Uhlfeld is a foreigner,
and a traitor to his own country; he may be

useful as a spy in war, but not as an honourable counsellor in peace; besides this, I cannot believe that your Majesty would insult an unfortunate King so far as to make him negotiate with a man who is his personal enemy."

" You are very bold, Count Tot," said Charles, " and perhaps you are thinking of your descent from King Erik; but recollect," he added harshly, " that I am King of Sweden."*

It may be imagined how keenly the King of Denmark felt his losses. One of his ministers, named Schel, fretted himself to death at the humiliation of his country; and another, who had to sign the treaty, told Meadows that he wished he could neither read nor write.

Frederick, however, supported his misfortunes with magnanimity, and received Charles at the castle of Fredericksborg with as much courtesy as if he had been entertaining a benefactor.

Charles was not to be disarmed with such weapons. He only intended by the treaty of Roskild to . escape the dangers of a coalition against him, and he never really meant to remain at peace.

* Fryxell. P. 37.

Wrangel received orders to remain in the Danish territory with his army, contrary to the terms of the treaty; but as Charles was too artful to allow any written evidence of his perfidy, he sent his confidant, Dahlberg, with a note to Wrangel, which ordered him to give implicit credence to what the bearer might tell him.

As it was necessary to give some account of his fresh preparations, he alternately circulated reports of an impending war with Poland, with Branden. burg, or with Russia.*

He amused the clergy with the prospect of another religious war against Austria; but the clergy had lost their zest for religious wars, since they had been called on to pay taxes. They advised him to seek peace, for peace was pleasing to God; and they reminded him that Sweden was exhausted both of men and of money.

They said that Gustavus Adolphus had been hailed as a deliverer in Germany, but that people now lived there happily, and that a fresh invader would be execrated as a public enemy.

* Meadows' Narrative. P 81.

† Engestrom, ' Ut drag ur Rosenhane's Dag Bok.' d 30 May 1658.

‡ Prestestandet's Archiv. Acta Comitialia, 1658.

When Charles's real intentions became known,
all his advisers endeavoured to dissuade him from
the fresh aggression on Denmark. Torlon warned
him that Louis XIV. would take it ill if he
violated a treaty so favourable to Sweden, and which
had been negotiated under the auspices of France.

Charles dissimulated to the last moment. The
day before he embarked with his army to invade
Denmark, he sent messages to Frederick which
expressed the warmest friendship and regard.

These messages were entrusted to a Danish
gentleman named Gabel, and his indignation at
Charles's treachery produced important results; for
he travelled day and night to Holland, and by his
vehement denunciations of the Swedish King,
persuaded the Dutch to hasten the departure of
their fleet.

Charles felt no scruples about the perfidious
attack he was about to make on his neighbour.
As he set sail he sang a Psalm, " In thee, O Lord,
is my trust."

Those who defended his conduct based their
arguments on the success which they anticipated.
They said, "We will conquer Denmark, and then
prove the justice of the war."

Contrary to their expectations, they did not conquer Denmark.

Copenhagen made one of those vigorous and successful defences which sometimes occur when a whole population is roused.

The Danes had but few regular troops, but they made fierce and successful sallies on the besiegers.

Nine hundred Swedes were killed in one of these skirmishes, and in another Charles only escaped by the swiftness of his horse.

A Danish officer followed him closely, and with loud taunts challenged him to stop, and prove his boasted valour hand to hand.

The Dutch were not inactive. On the 28th of October their fleet passed the Sound, midway between the hostile castles, and commenced a furious battle with the Swedish ships.

The English navy was the only one which could match the Dutch at this time. The Swedes were completely defeated, and Copenhagen received supplies of provisions and a reinforcement of Dutch troops.

The mediation of England, France, and Holland was again offered, and haughtily rejected by

Charles. The Dutch consequently landed some troops in Fyen, who effected a junction with the Danes and totally defeated the Swedes.

There was no escape for the vanquished army, as the hostile fleet surrounded the island, and the heroes of a hundred fights were obliged to lay down their arms.

After this, negotiations began again. The celebrated Algernon Sidney was the representative of England, and he was foremost in checking the arrogance of Charles. The only result of so much violence and injustice, and of so many burdens laid upon Sweden, was to leave her in a worse position than she stood in before the commencement of the war; and Charles began to be considered the general enemy of Europe. His reverses affected both his health and spirits. His constitution had never been very strong, and was much injured by his constant hardships.

Wounded pride finished what disease had begun, and a few days' illness gave a peace to the North which would have been very uncertain so long as Charles Gustavus lived.

He spoke some time to his sister, Maria Euphrosyne, about the administration during his son's minority; then, heaving a deep sigh, said, " Fyen, my sister, the loss of Fyen kills me ! "

He died on the 13th of February, 1660.

The war had interfered very much with Christina's revenues. Her income was chiefly drawn from Pomerania, but towns plundered by the enemy were not in a condition to keep engagements which had been made in time of peace.

Christina had already sold her plate and jewels, when the Pope came to the rescue of his convert, and assigned her a pension of 12,000 scudi.

He also induced her to appoint Cardinal Azzolini the general manager of her affairs. The Cardinal was not only a man of taste and learning, but also a good man of business. He introduced a degree of method and economy to which Christina's affairs had been little accustomed, and she was again left free to pursue her literary inclinations.

About this time she paid a good deal of attention to the study and practice of chemistry, but that branch of knowledge was in so low a state in the seventeenth century that her efforts were necessarily crude and empirical.

Christina took her part in the costly and desultory experiments which were then in vogue, and she

was with some reason accused of turning a considerable part of her revenues into smoke.   It was
necessary that these rude essays should precede
any true knowledge of the science, and those
students deserve their share of honour who perceived
the grandeur of their subject through all the clouds
of error and absurdity; who recognized the pure
gold through all the mass of alloy.

The seed sown bore fruit in the next century, when
two Swedes, Bergmann and Scheele, were among
the first who made any real progress in chemistry.

The Roman Pontiff no doubt expected that
Christina would be a more obedient daughter when
she became his pensionary, and in some respects
he was not disappointed.

She persuaded some of her Swedish followers to
change their religion, and amongst the rest her
secretary, Davidson.

When she sent him to Charles Gustavus about
her arrears, the King made his own piety an excuse
for avoiding inconvenient claims, and refused to
see the envoy unless he took an oath that he was
not a Catholic.

Davidson informed Christina of the dilemma he
was in, and she replied—

Christina was believed to be partial to the French faction at Rome, and to encourage the enlisting of troops against Naples. The Pope, consequently, to her great indignation, placed sentries round her palace to watch her proceedings.

It was while matters were in this state that she received tidings of the death of Charles Gustavus.

The late King's brother, Duke Adolphus, made the announcement to her, and at the same time informed her that he had been named one of the Regents.

Christina replied,—

" My cousin,—Although during the late King's life I had sometimes reason to be dissatisfied with his conduct, yet I always preserved for him that friendship and affection of which he received such memorable proofs. This friendship causes me to lament his death, especially as it happened at a time when I expected an alteration in his conduct, favourable to myself. But as we must submit, without murmuring, to the will of God, I will not give way to useless complaints, but hope that God will console us for our loss by other benefits.

" I thank you for your kind letter, and assure you that you will find in me such a disposition as

"It appears to me that honour and life are two things worthy of care. If you deny or dissemble your religion, you will save neither.

"Do not let the King's menaces frighten you; come back to me without seeing him—come without having done anything base, and prove to me that you have lived like a good Catholic. If you return in this way I will receive you with joy, and if I have only a morsel of bread I will divide it with you; but if fear makes you neglect your duty do not expect to see me again, and be sure that I will punish you, and that all the power of the King of Sweden shall not hinder me." *

Subjects of dispute, however, arose between the Pope and the Queen.

One of the first was about her favourite, Count Sentinelli. Christina wished to arrange a marriage between him and the Duchess de Ceri, the richest heiress in Rome.

The Pope stopped her match-making in a very summary way; he obliged the Duchess to enter a convent, and he banished Sentinelli from Rome. The harmony once disturbed between the two personages, their disputes soon became frequent.

* 'Catteau Calleville.' Tome II. P 66.

Christina was believed to be partial to the French faction at Rome, and to encourage the enlisting of troops against Naples. The Pope, consequently, to her great indignation, placed sentries round her palace to watch her proceedings.

It was while matters were in this state that she received tidings of the death of Charles Gustavus.

The late King's brother, Duke Adolphus, made the announcement to her, and at the same time informed her that he had been named one of the Regents.

Christina replied,—

" My cousin,—Although during the late King's life I had sometimes re ison to be dissatisfied with his conduct, yet I always preserved for him that friendship and affection of which he received such memorable proofs. This friendship causes me to lament his death, especially as it happened at a time when I expected an alteration in his conduct, favourable to myself. But as we must submit, without murmuring, to the will of God, I will not give way to useless complaints, but hope that God will console us for our loss by other benefits.

" I thank you for your kind letter, and assure you that you will find in me such a disposition as

you wish, to maintain a good understanding w i
the King my nephew and with his mother.

" I congratulate you on the office which the
late King has entrusted to you, of assisting in the
education of his son. You will gratify me by ac-
quitting yourself well in this duty. Any one else
might exhort you to remind the young King of
what I have done for him, but I shall consider
myself repaid for everything if he recollects what
he owes to Sweden.

" Endeavour to teach him his duty, and to
make him seek his glory in the good of his country
and in the happiness of his people. Render him
worthy of my throne, and that of his ancestors ;
teach him to fill our place worthily, and inspire
him with a noble emulation of the great and
heroic deeds of the King my father . . . . The
change in the orders concerning myself since the
King's death leads me to think that if he had lived
he would have become more favourable to me. I
attribute to the Queen Dowager the orders which
have been given concerning the payment of my
revenue; I pray you thank her for me, and
assure her that I wish to honour and serve her the
same as if she were my own sister.

" I request you to observe that I am about to come to a place where I may be of more use to their Majesties, and where I hope to settle my claims. I give you this information in the conviction that you will be glad of it, and that you will assist mé by your good offices with the Queen, so that I may at last experience the fulfilment of the many promises with which I have been hitherto amused. . . . . Recollect the gratitude which you owe to Sweden for having given a crown to your house. The wars of the late King show that it is not such an easy thing, as is sometimes supposed, to conquer a kingdom, and should make you esteem all the more the favour your family has received from Sweden.—Rome, June 12, 1660."*

As she hinted in this letter, she determined to visit Sweden immediately, in the first place to get her revenues confirmed to her by the new government, and next to assert her own claims in case the reigning family, which was now only represented by a boy eight years old, should become extinct.

The Queen Dowager, the Swedish nobles, and the French Government took alarm at her projected visit, and Mazarin accused her to the Senate

* Archenholtz. Tome II., p.p. 36, 37

of visiting Sweden for the purpose of introducing
the Catholic religion.   This was untrue, and came
with a bad grace from a Cardinal of the Roman
Church ; but it supplied the Swedish nobles with
an excuse, and gained them the assistance of the
Lutheran Clergy, with whom they were at variance
about the appointment of Duke Adolphus as
Regent.

The disputes in the Diet about Duke Adolphus
were so violent as almost to cause a civil war, and
as Christina was decidedly against the Duke, her
cousin, it is necessary to say something of his
conduct and character, and for this purpose to
anticipate the order of time.

Charles Gustavus had determined, some years
before, to leave his brother Adolphus, Grand
Marshal and Regent in case of his own death,
but not without some misgivings that Adolphus
might be such another uncle as Charles IX.
had been to Sigismund.

He resolved to name Magnus de la Gardie also
a Regent and Chancellor of the kingdom, because,
on account of his foreign extraction, he was less
likely to join the high nobles in their schemes
against the royal authority.

The King named in his will, as the other Regents, Brahe, Wrangel, and Herman Fleming, and desired that his widow, Hedvig Eleonora, should have two votes in the Council.

The appointment of his brother as Grand Marshal and Regent was a great proof of Charles Gustavus's want of judgment.

It was illegal for any one but a native-born Swede to hold either of these offices.

The character of the Duke was a still stronger objection, and justified the extreme measures which the leading members in the Senate were prepared to take to enforce his exclusion.

His own domain of Katrinenburg was managed with such violence and injustice as to be almost depopulated. After Charles XI. assumed the government he ordered his uncle to change his governor, and threatened, as the alternative, to take the administration into his own hands.* The Duke then left Sweden and went to Austria, where he made himself so obnoxious that he was forbidden the Court.

On his return to Sweden he had a law-suit with Stenbock, in which a decision was given against

* Riksregistratur. Karl den Elfte till Adolf Johan. d. 7 April, 1673.

the Duke. He then addressed a notice to the Nobles, Bishops and Council, in which he denied the jurisdiction of the Swedish Courts, or of the King himself.

The Duke's behaviour to his own family was the worst of all his faults. They grew up in his castle at Stegdorg without a single friend or companion. The two princesses, twenty-six and twenty-four years of age, were kept prisoners. The young princes were constantly treated with blows.

The unfortunate family wrote secretly to entreat the King's interference; but as even the royal remonstrances had no effect, they escaped altogether, one night, from their prison, and reached Stockholm exhausted and half naked. Adolphus sent his servants to recapture them, and when this plan failed, announced his intention of fetching them himself.

Charles XI. sent an officer to desire him to remain at home, as they would not be given up to so unnatural a parent.

The Duke sent an insolent answer, in which he said he would cite Charles before the Emperor.*

* Riksregistratur. Karl den Elfte till Adolf Johan. d. 18 Juli, 1673.

The King at last discovered a means of bringing his uncle to his senses; the young princes and princesses were kept at Stockholm, and the Duke's pension was stopped until he submitted.

Such was the conduct of Duke Adolphus to his superiors, and to his own family, and as may be supposed he was violent and tyrannical in the extreme to those beneath him; yet his claims to the regency were not set aside without a hard struggle. The clergy were all along in his favour, and for some time they succeeded in gaining the support of the peasants. The nobles opposed the Duke's nomination most vehemently, and they won over the Queen Dowager to their side.

After a violent contest, in which an appeal to arms was threatened more than once, the Diet agreed to exclude Duke Adolphus.

Five Regents were appointed, as in the time of Christina's minority. The Queen Dowager was allowed two votes, in deference to the late King's wish, but Herman Fleming was excluded from his office because he was a partisan of Adolphus. The Duke's only other adherent among the nobles was Banér, nicknamed Dulle (the stupid).

It was in a great measure through the exertions

of Brahe that the matter was settled, and Christina wrote him a flattering letter, in which she called him the Saviour of his country, and requested his support for her just claims.

She did not show her usual penetration in this, for Brahe was in fact her bitterest enemy. She had injured herself and Sweden by her excessive liberality to the nobles, yet they were ever false to her, and she now erred in imputing to patriotism the measures which they only took for their own interests.

Not long after Christina thus expressed her admiration for Brahe, he proposed that she should be " sent to Aland, in the charge of an honourable and determined man."

De la Gardie answered, " This would be very like taking her prisoner."

" Yes," said Brahe, " that is just what I mean, and it would be the best thing for her."*

Christina arrived at Hamburg the 18th of August, and was received by the magistrates and chief citizens, and by the foreign ministers, among whom were Terlon and Algernon Sidney.

* Rådsprot. d 21 Juli, 1668. Apud Fryxell. Vol. XIV. P. 22.

She soon found out that she would not be alto
gether welcome in Sweden, and she wrote to Mr.
Bååt, the governor-general of her domains: "Although your letter intimates that my arrival is not
desired, I beg that you will satisfy the Regents of
my intentions, and assure all good Swedes that
they would be wrong to prevent me from coming,
and that my presence will be useful to the State.
—21st Aug. 1660."

The man who most objected to her return, was
her old favourite, Magnus de la Gardie. He and
his party determined that Baron Linde should be
sent to meet her, and request she would not come
to Stockholm until the Diet was over. Linde
was authorized, if necessary, to employ force to
prevent her further advance.

She landed in Sweden the 17th of September,
and was immediately presented with a letter from
Brahe, which requested her not to come to Stockholm, to which she replied:

"My cousin, I esteem everything from you so
much, that I cannot feel offended by you. I am
exceedingly sorry to find myself in a position
where I cannot honourably follow your advice."

Linde, the son of her old nurse, was rather

ashamed of his employment; he did not venture to stop Christina; and although the Council were angry at his disobedience, she was still so popular that they dared not take any violent measure.

Her first act was to send a memorial to the Diet, asking for the confirmation of her revenues, and the payment of her arrears.

The other orders were disposed to admit her claims without any opposition; but the clergy demanded time for consideration.

After the lapse of some days they were pressed for an answer, when the remark they made discovered the spirit by which they were actuated. They said, " The Queen has had four or five years to prepare her claims, she may surely allow the clergy as many days to examine them."

In the meantime they stirred up the public discontent at her Catholic suite, and preached against her from their pulpits.

When they thought that the opinions of the other orders had been sufficiently set against the Queen, they sent in their answer.

They said that she was now Christina Allessandra, a Catholic, and not the same person to whom the grant had been made in 1654; she could therefore no longer have any legal claim to her revenues, and if they were continued it could only be in remembrance of her ancestor's virtues.

The other orders agreed in this decision, and Brahe thanked the clergy for their orthodox zeal.

Encouraged by the public approval of their magnanimity, the bishops and clergy visited Christina the same day, and informed her that she could no longer be permitted to take part in the Catholic service. The old Archbishop Lenœus spoke so harshly to her that she burst into tears, and the proud Queen begged in vain on her knees that some indulgence might be extended to the Catholics.*

The Lutheran clergy were relentless, and old Lenœus continued his reproaches.

* Sveriges Historia, under Konungarne af Pfalziska Huset. Kap. vi.

'Nous trouvons en termes très-exprès que celni qui se départira de notre doctrine, et embrassera la Papistique perdra ses héritages, droits, et avantages par tout le Roïaume de Suède. Tontefois nous consentons que Sa Majesté jonisse de ses ɟhiens et revenus accordés, non en vertu du Recès fait à la resignation de sa couronne, mais purement en considération de sa réputation, et des grands mérites de ses Ancêtres envers la couronne de Suède.'—Archenholtz, Tome II., p. 45.

"We know very well," he said, "what the Pope wants; we know his zeal to get our souls."

" I know the Pope better than you do," said the outraged Queen. " He would not give four dollars for all your souls put together."

One of her former Chaplains now asked her rudely why she had fallen away from the true faith. Christina answered : " It was your long and stupid sermons that disgusted me."

A few days after this her chapel was pulled down by order of the Senate, and her Catholic attendants were banished.

Christina then went to the Catholic service at the residence of Terlon, and had a certificate sent to Rome to say that she had duly attended the rites of her church at the holy season of Easter.

Although she was never the least inclined to fanaticism, she carefully attended the ordinances of her religion, in spite of all intimidation, and she deliberately risked the success of her other schemes, rather than flinch from what she considered her religious duty.

The reception of her memorial about her revenues was not encouraging ; notwithstanding which, she shortly afterwards gave each of the orders a copy of the claim which she asserted, under certain circumstances, to the throne.

She said that when she abdicated in 1654, she had not contemplated the early death of Charles Gustavus. The heir to the throne was now a delicate child, only eight years old. If anything should happen to him, the branch of the family in which the crown was settled would become extinct. Such an event might cause great troubles, and even civil war, in Sweden.

Her present declaration was intended to prevent such a catastrophe. Her renunciation had been in favour of Charles Gustavus and his legitimate heirs. If these should fail, the crown ought to revert to her.

This proposal was rejected by all the States, and she was obliged to sign another act of renunciation. Magnus de la Gardie, now become the Chancellor, was sent to demand her signature, and she had no choice but to submit. She was in the power of the Senate and Council, and had perhaps heard a whisper of their intention to imprison her for life.

It cannot be denied that there was some justice in her proposal, and that it was calculated to avert, or, at least, to postpone, the evils of a disputed succession; but the Swedish nobles were not inclined to part with the power they had unexpectedly gained.*

For some years after this, the aristocracy ruled Sweden without opposition; but the really great men had disappeared, and the views of the present rulers were selfish and paltry.

The peace of Oliva, signed in 1660, ought to have restored prosperity to Sweden, and it removed all anxiety on the side of Poland, which formally resigned her claims to the crown of the Vasas. Nothing was done, however, for the improvement of the country.

Under the administration of Magnus de la Gardie, the finances were bankrupt, and the Swedish arms met with defeat and disgrace.

Terserus, the Bishop of Abo, thought the rejection of her memorial a favourable opportunity for

† Algernon Sidney, who was well acquainted with Swedish politics, shrewdly observed, ' Independently of the aversion they have for her religion, there is no government which the Senate and Nobles of Sweden like so much as the minority of their kings. They were obliged to submit to the King; but now the power is in their own hands.'—Sidney's letter to Lord Leicester. Archenholtz, Vol. IV., p. 262.

attacking Christina in a fresh way, and he wrote letters to Germany, in which he asserted that she repented of her change of religion, and that he had seen her weeping on this account.

Christina resented this malignant attempt to make the Pope regard her with suspicion, and she dwelt justly on the ingratitude of Terserus, whose life she had spared when it was forfeited by the part he took in the conspiracy of Messenius.

As she found it necessary to remain in Sweden until her affairs were settled, she withdrew to the castle of Norköping, which was situate in her own domains, and where she expected she could exercise her religion without molestation. The animosity of the Lutheran clergy followed her even here. They first proposed to imprison her, and when they could not prevail on the Government to adopt this measure, they procured an order to forbid the exercise of her religion.

Christina wrote an eloquent letter to the governor of her domains on this subject, which showed the injustice, illegality, and folly of this prohibition, and which had the effect of making the Senate ashamed of being so completely the tools of the clergy. She said—

" Mr. Bååt,—I am astonished at this proceeding of the Government; and, feeling that I deserve
better treatment, I make a last attempt to soften
the malice of my enemies. Pray communicate
with the Senate, and remind them that, if I receive an affront, it will be more disgrace to them
than to me. If foreign ministers had not this
privilege, I would not complain; but it is repug-
nant to reason, to the law of nations, and to all
law, that I should be worse treated than the most
insignificant foreign envoy.

" I can only oppose violence by entreaties, but
remind them of their own honour, and also that,
however unfortunate I may be, I can never become
their subject.

" If they leave me alone, I shall every day con-
firm the promise I made, to resign all future pretensions, because the profession of the Catholic
religion is sufficient to preclude all hope of gaining
anything in Sweden.

" For heaven's sake send me my money, that I
may leave a country where I am so cruelly persecuted. . . . I wait your answer, and if they
violate all rights, both human and divine, and forget what is due to me, I will bear the affront with

such patience as to turn it to my own glory and to their shame.

*   *   *   *   *

" If you have any regard for me, arrange my affairs in such a way that I may get away from here, for I declare to you, upon my honour, I will not remain an hour after they are settled.— Norköping, 7th March, 1661."*

This letter appears to have had the desired effect, for Christina left Sweden shortly after this, and reached Hamburg the 16th of May.

She remained there a whole year, and placed the management of her affairs in the hands of a rich banker named Texeira.

From his statement, it appears that she only received 107,000 dollars a-year from Sweden, instead of 200,000, to which she was entitled.

As remonstrances did not bring more money, Christina endeavoured to increase her revenues by alchemy.

An adventurer, named Borri, was then residing

* Archenholtz. Tome II., p. 58.

in Hamburg. He had been accused of heresy in Italy, and fled for his life from that country.

Christina took him under her patronage, and listened to his fables about the transmutation of metals; but her credulity was not so unlimited as he desired. He left Hamburg suddenly, and gave out that he did not like Christina well enough to impart his secrets to her.

He then went to Denmark, and Frederick III. spent large sums of money in the hope of being more favoured; but, as the manufacture of gold did not progress, Borri set out for Turkey, in the hope of duping the Sultan.

On his way through Germany, he was arrested on suspicion of being concerned in some conspiracy. He explained the object of his journey, but, unfortunately, the report which would have exculpated him, was made in the presence of the Papal Nuncio.

The vengeance of the churchman was roused at the name of Borri. He claimed the prisoner on behalf of the Holy See, and the Emperor gave him up on condition that his life should be spared.

Borri ended his days in the Castle of St. Angelo, and did not succeed in making gold.

Christina had a worthier protégé at Hamburg, the learned Lambecius.

He was the object of public persecution on account of his religious opinions, and his home was made wretched by an avaricious and ill-tempered wife.

Christina persuaded him to leave Hamburg, and to become a Roman Catholic. He remained some time at Rome; after which he went to Vienna, and became librarian to the Emperor.

Lambecius was more grateful than most of her favourites, and continued to write Latin and Greek verses in honour of Christina.

On her return to Rome, her palace became more than ever the centre of attraction to the learned. Any scholar could get access to her books, manuscripts, and cabinets.

She read everything worthy of notice that was published, and encouraged the authors.

The academy which she founded, flourished after her death, and bore fruits over all Italy.

Her taste for art was animated by her residence in the city which was its home; nor did she lavish all her admiration on the old masters, to the exclusion of those who were labouring to rival them.

The artists valued her cordial appreciation even more than her patronage.

Bernini, who was called the modern Michael Angelo, made a statue of Christ, which she refused to buy, because she said 'she could not give any sum at all equal to its value.

When the great sculptor died, he left Christina the gem she so greatly admired.*

Her active mind could not help sometimes employing itself in political affairs.

She was strongly impressed with the dangers to be apprehended from the fanaticism and the military power of the Turks, and she employed Count Galeazzo Gualdo to visit the principal courts of Europe for the purpose of forming a league against the Moslem.

Her efforts were unsuccessful, but the accuracy of her judgment was proved a few years later, when the Turks invaded Germany and carried off as slaves many of the noblest families.

There was then no adequate force to resist them, and it was only the extraordinary courage and good fortune of Sobieski which saved a consider-

* Biographie Universelle.—Art. Bernini.

able part of Europe from being subjugated by the barbarous invaders.

Soon after Christina's return to Rome, the Pope had a serious quarrel with Louis XIV.

The Duke de Créqui, the French Ambassador at Rome, was insolent and overbearing.

His suite imitated his behaviour. They frequently raised tumults in the streets, and on one occasion they made a furious attack on a party of the Corsican Guards, who formed the police of the city.

The Corsicans got the worst in the fray, and they determined to gratify their national taste for revenge.

They besieged the Palace Farnese, where the Duke resided, and opened a brisk fire of musketry on the windows.

The Duke showed himself on a balcony, but instead of respecting his office, the Corsicans continued the attack with increased animation.

During the assault the Duchess returned to the Palace. The Corsicans fired on her carriage, killed one of her suite, and wounded several others The Duchess was obliged to take refuge with the Cardinal D'Este, and it was by good fortune alone

that she and her husband escaped with their lives.

The Pope was not at first very willing to give satisfaction for this outrage, and Christina endeavoured to exercise her favourite office of peacemaker. She wrote several letters to Louis XIV., begging him to moderate his indignation, but her interference was not well received; and as the Pope did not at once concede all that was required of him, Louis seized upon Avignon, and prepared some troops to march into Italy. The Pope was obliged to send his nephew, Cardinal Chigi, to apologize, the Corsican guard was disbanded, and a monument was erected in Rome to commemorate the insult and reparation.

When hostilities seemed impending between France and the Holy See, Christina announced her intention of returning to Sweden, and although war was averted by the submission of the weaker power, she continued the preparations for her departure.

Many conjectures were made as to the secret objects she might have in view.

One opinion was, that her astrological advisers had predicted the approaching death of the young

King, and that she wished to be on the spot to take advantage of such an event.

The old clamour was also renewed about her desire to introduce the Catholic religion into Sweden, and this motive has been attributed to her by the very persons who accused her of indifference to her new religion. It is not uncommon for opposite factions to accuse a moderate person both of fanaticism and of indifference, but it was Christina's strange fate to be charged by the same writers with these contradictory faults.

The truth is that she expressed herself decidedly averse to the plans proposed in Rome and in Paris, of sending a number of Jesuits to Sweden. "It would be the same thing," she said, "as sending them to death; and as for converting the regular Swedish Lutherans, it is an absolute impossibility."*

She left Rome the latter end of the year 1666, and remained some time in Hamburg.

She went one day to examine a fine collection of medals which belonged to a Mr. Luders. She ac-

---

* 'Det ar detsamma som at skicka dem till galgen, sade Kristina, ty at omvända de strängt Lutherska vrenskarna, är en fullkomlig omojlighet.' Fryxell. Tionde Delen. P. 288.

cidentally took up the one which commemorated her abdication. The reverse of the medal represented a crown, with the inscription " Et sine te."

When she perceived what it was, she threw it angrily on the table, and it was easy to see that her sentiments were changed with regard to the crown.

Her old rivals the Danes treated her with the utmost courtesy and respect. A magnificent barge was prepared for her at Cronberg, the fort and all the ships saluted her, and it was not until she reached Sweden that she was treated with any want of consideration.

The Regents felt, or pretended to feel, considerable alarm at Christina's approach.

They issued a proclamation in May, 1667, which forbade her the exercise of the Catholic religion during her stay. She was forbidden to be present at any meeting of the States, and the Regents announced that it would be necessary to take extraordinary precautions about the young King's health.

The young Count Pontus de la Gardie was sent to meet Christina at Helsingborg, and to escort her to Stockholm.

She had not proceeded further than Jonköping when a courier brought the Count orders to inform the Queen that she must dismiss the Roman Catholic priest who attended her, or that he would be proceeded against according to law. Christina expressed her determination not to submit to this affront, and said that as her priest was obliged to leave the country, she would leave it with him. Although it was nearly midnight at the time, she gave orders to prepare for her instant departure. De la Gardie had more gentlemanlike feeling than his employers, and was ashamed of the part he was obliged to play.

He entreated Christina to delay her departure until he could communicate and remonstrate with the Regents.

A courier was despatched to Stockholm, and the Queen advanced as far as Norköping to wait there for the answer.

All that the Regents desired was an excuse for stopping Christina's journey, and the pretext of religion was thought likely to be more popular than any other.

The answer sent to De la Gardie was even more peremptory than the order he had just received.

He was instructed to acquaint the Queen that the Regents would not relax their previous determination, and moreover that she would not be permitted to attend mass at the house of any of the foreign ambassadors.

The day after she received this communication Christina began to retrace her steps, having previously dismissed the suite who had been sent to attend upon her, and whose services she declined any longer to accept. The feelings of these attendants were so little in accordance with those of their masters, that many of them parted from her with tears, and the people of Norköping evinced the same sympathy and sorrow.*

At the towns she passed through on her return the people surrounded her carriage, and expressed their grief with tears and lamentations.

They said that when she ruled the country it was crowned with all kinds of blessing, but that it was now oppressed with every sort of misfortune.†

---

* Archenholtz. Tome II. P. 115.

† 'De försakrade, att medan drottningen regerade, var landet bekrőt med all slags välsignelse, nu deremot belastadt med all slags vedervårdighet.'—Rådsprot, d. 8 Aug., 1667. Fryxell.

Pontus de la Gardie himself, at his own particular request, accompanied her as far as Helsingborg, but he afterwards complained bitterly of the rate at which she travelled, and was confined to his bed, from the effects of the fatigue, for several days after his arrival at Helsingborg.

It was a sharp journey even for a young Swedish soldier, as the whole distance from Norköping to Helsingborg (nearly 300 miles) was accomplished in four days.

When Christina took leave of the Count, she said, " Tell the King that my pride will keep me from complaining, and my patriotism will prevent me from seeking revenge."

The result of Christina's journey was favourable to her. The Regents and Council were generally blamed for their harsh and uncourteous behaviour. The States, and even the clergy, became better disposed to her, and the nobles alone rejoiced at her departure.*

She had displayed a steadiness of purpose, without bigotry, which could hardly fail to win respect.

---

* Some of them said, ' Vill hon ej bida så må hon gerna rida.' ' If she will not bide, she is welcome to ride.'

She said that if she wore the crown again she would never oblige any one to change his religion, and that she would say, like Turenne, " I am a Catholic, but my sword is Protestant."

Christina returned to Hamburg in June, 1667. Here she received news of the death of Alexander VII.

It was rumoured at the same time that Cardinal Farnese was likely to succeed him, and as Christina had not been on good terms with Farnese, she appears to have been in doubt whether she should return to Rome.   At one time she thought of residing at Venice, or else of remaining at Hamburg.

· Presently the agreeable tidings arrived of Cardinal Rospigliosi's election, under the name of Clement IX.

The new pontiff had always been friendly to Christina, and his cheerful, amiable disposition promised to make her residence at Rome more pleasant than ever.

Unfortunately she determined to manifest her satisfaction in a manner which was very injudicious whilst she was a visitor in a Protestant country.

On the evening of the 15th of July, her residence was illuminated, and fireworks represented the arms of Clement IX., and the triumph of the Roman Church over heresy. The populace were further excited by an act of liberality, which, without its obnoxious accompaniments, would have gratified them. Fountains of wine flowed in frout of her hotel; and the people at first drank to Christina's health.

Presently, however, they took offence at some transparencies of the same nature as the fireworks.

Stimulated by the wine, and by some Lutheran clergy, they broke the transparencies, and then attacked the guard.

The soldiers fired on the crowd, and killed or wounded a considerable number.

The sturdy population, composed of artisans and seamen, were exasperated, instead of being intimidated by this violence. It was soon found that the guard could not hold its ground against the increasing numbers and energy of the assailants, and Christina was obliged to escape in disguise to the house of the Swedish ambassador.

In the meantime the commandant of the city

sent some troops to the spot, and the mob dispersed quietly before an authority which they recognized.

The whole affair was more creditable to the people of Hamburg than to the Queen : they were so placable, that the very next day she passed through the crowds collected at the spot, without meeting any opposition or insult. Christina distributed a considerable sum of money among the sufferers, but it does not appear that she made any apology for her conduct, or that the authorities took any official notice of it, although she remained nearly a year in Hamburg after this unfortunate occurrence.

The Swedish Diet met in 1668, and Christina remained in Hamburg to wait the result of her negotiations.

Rosenbach was sent as her envoy to the States as well as to the Regents.

He requested permission for her to enter Sweden, and to practise her religion during her residence in that country.

He also asked for the arrears which were due to her, and proposed to exchange her domains in Pomerania for the Duchy of Bremen.

There was much more disposition at this time to concede her claims, than there had been the last year. The nobles were now almost alone in their animosity, and even among them there was some difference of opinion.

Brahe and De la Gardie were the most bitter against her. The former renewed his advice that she should be imprisoned in Öland, if she came to Sweden.

Magnus de la Gardie approved of the proposal, and said that Charles Gustavus had intended to shut her up, if she had come to Sweden in his time,* but as the new Chancellor had never been famous for truthfulness, it may be hoped that Charles Gustavus never contemplated an act of such baseness.

The proposal to imprison her was not a secret altogether confined to the Council.

Algernon Sidney had a conversation with Christina at Hamburg, and told her that she ought to have some guarantee before she ventured into Sweden again. He remarked that although most of the Senate owed their fortunes to her, it was very probable that if they had her in their

* Fryxell. Tionde Delen. P. 301.

the country.

H

pped to
the D

There was much more disposition at this time to concede her claims, than there had been the last year. The nobles were now almost alone in their animosity, and even among them there was some difference of opinion.

Brahe and De la Gardie were the most bitter against her. The former renewed his advice that she should be imprisoned in Oland, if she came into Sweden.

Magnus de la Gardie approved of the plan, and said that Charles Gustavus would certainly shut her up, if she had come over in time,* but as the new Chancellor was famous for truthfulness, it can _ro- Charles Gustavus never contemplated _ its such baseness.

The proposal to imprison _ith the altogether confined to the Council. ully ob- should be

Algernon Sidney _ allowed to Christina at Hamburg _ her suite, ought to have some _ ise of their into S_

le no use of the Azzolini at Florence.

power, she might pass the rest of her life in some Swedish castle, instead of in her palace at Rome.*

Christina's trusty adviser and friend, Azzolini, also apprehended real danger to her in the event of a visit to Sweden. It is pretty certain that the men who ruled there would not have been deterred by any feeling of justice or honour, although they might have been restrained by fear of the indignation of the States at such an act.

Christina affected to despise these warnings, but it is uncertain how far she was influenced by them, and how far they caused her to abandon her projected visit to Sweden.

Her answer to Azzolini betokens a degree of melancholy which does not often appear in her letters. It is dated Hamburg, the 20th May, 1668 :—

" You are wrong to find fault with my proposed journey to Sweden. All that I have told you of that country is true, and I assure you that opinion is as favourable to me there as possible. Those who rule, indeed, fear and hate me, but the people love me, my fortune, and my renown.

* Sidney's Letter to Lord Leicester. 8th Sept., 1660.

" Time will give you the proof of this. For myself I will not dispute with you about it, but beg you to examine the reports you receive from others more disinterested than myself.

" It is still quite possible that some dangers may attend the journey, but I assure you that no love for life will prevent me from venturing, for I have lost everything that could make life pleasant, and the last day of my life will certainly be the happiest."*

Christina's opinion of the affection borne her by the people was justified by the conduct of the States.

They also had reason to complain of the arrogance of the Council, and they overruled its decisions about Christina.

They decreed that the agreement made with the Queen at her abdication should be faithfully observed ; that the arrears of her revenues should be paid within a year; that she should be allowed to visit Sweden ; and that she, with all her suite, should be allowed the free exercise of their religion.

It appears strange that she made no use of the

* Letter in collection of the Marquis Azzolini at Florence.

victory for which she had so long contended. She gave up her intended journey to Sweden, and prepared for her return to Rome.

It was supposed that Azzolini's warning had something to do with her change of plan; but the chief motive for her journey was the desire to secure her revenue, and when this was accomplished, she may have been unwilling to cause a rupture between the Council and the States. She also had a scheme about this time, to gain another throne which had been in the Vasa family, and which was now about to become vacant.

On the 16th of September, 1668, John Casimir addressed the assembled nobles, clergy, and people, as follows :—

" Poles ! two hundred and eighty years have passed since my family first mounted your throne. The rule of my family ceases with me. Worn out by the fatigues of war, by care, and by age, exhansted by a difficult reign of twenty-one years, your King returns to you all that the world esteems most brilliant. He returns you the crown which you gave him.

" In future, instead of a throne, I shall only want a few inches of earth to rejoin my ancestors.

" It was your love for me which raised me to the highest rank; my love for you makes me resign this great dignity.

" If I have offended some of you, I entreat you to consider that the misfortunes of the times alone were the cause, and I ask you to forgive offences which did not proceed from my will, as sincerely as I forgive all who have offended me. Though I may reside far from Poland, my thoughts will always remain with you, and with this feeling in my heart, it is my last desire that my ashes may repose among you."

Thus, by a singular coincidence, the last of their race in two branches of the Vasa family, both resigned a crown, and went to die among strangers.

Christina returned to Rome the 22nd of November, 1668, and received a cordial and magnificent welcome from Clement IX.

Fifty carriages, each drawn by six horses, formed part of the procession. The Horse Guards met her ten miles out of Rome, and the Swiss Guards waited for her at the Porto del Popolo.

Christina had commenced some negotiations about the Polish Crown before she left Hamburg as John Casimir's intention to abdicate was generally known at that time.

On her return to Rome, she sent her Chaplain Father Hacki, on a mission to Warsaw.

The Papal Nuncio was desired to give his assistance, and Clement wrote himself to the Polish Diet, and recommended Christina as the worthiest of the candidates for their throne.

He reminded them that she was the last scion of the ancient race which had worn the crowns of Sweden and of Poland, and thatshewould neverhave left the kingdom she inherited, if Sweden had been a Catholic country. It would be an injustice to her if they placed a stranger of less worth than herself on the throne of her ancestors.

Christina adroitly converted the objections to her celibacy, into arguments in her favour.

She said that, by leaving her free, the Poles would preserve their own liberty, because, after her death, they would not be tied to a particular family; and as she had no children to divide her affections, their happiness and glory would be her only objects.

The Poles thought that a very clever or a very powerful sovereign might rivet a heavier yoke on their necks than they were inclined to bear. They therefore rejected Christina, as well as the Czar of Russia and the great Condé, and they elected Michel Wienowitski, a private gentleman, and a native of Poland.

The new King had but little ambition or ability, and he was sufficiently acquainted with the character of his countrymen to foresee the troubles that awaited him.

He received the news of his elevation with alarm instead of pleasure, and he even shed tears at the prospects which others had so earnestly desired.

Christina bore her disappointment with dignity. Hacki received her orders to congratulate the new King, and to attend his coronation. Her pride might have prevented her from showing any annoyance, but it redounds to her credit that she never expressed any dissatisfacton with Hacki, but continued her favour to him as long as she lived.

After the contest for the Polish election, Christina was not so much engaged in political affairs, but she never altogether attained that philosophical ease and tranquillity which she had so fondly expected.

She had still an unfailing source of consolation

in her love of literature, nor did she draw on the intellectual wealth of others without making a full return.

One of the chief objects of the Academy she founded at Rome, was to cultivate a pure style, in opposition to the turgid and inflated productions which were then prevalent.

By this means she was enabled to exercise a greater influence on public taste than has often fallen to the lot of an individual.*

"It is said that productions of this Academy, which still exist in the Albani library, show the singular combination of essays in pure Tuscan by Italian Abbati, which owe their elegance to emendations from the hand of a Northern Queen."†

The rules of the Academy were well calculated to promote the object she had in view.

* 'I think we may even venture to affirm that Christina herself, when her character and intellect had been improved and matured, exerted a powerfully efficient and enduring influence on the period, more particularly on Italian literature.' —Ranke's 'History of the Popes.' Vol. II., p. 369.

'Rome was to poetry in this age, what Florence had once been, though Rome had hitherto done less for the Italian muses than any great city. Nor was this so much due to her bishops and cardinals, as to a stranger and a woman.'— Hallam's 'Lit. of Europe.' Vol. III., p. 468.

† Ranke. Vol. II., p. 370.

It was professed to be founded for the purpose of considering every subject that was pleasant, learned, and curious; for cultivating and improving the mind, the talents, and the language.

Every discourse was to be in Italian, and every speaker was enjoined to make his speech as clear, pure, and short as possible, as the aim was to cultivate learning unmixed with pedantry, and eloquence free from affectation.

Adulation and panegyric (especially of the Queen) were strictly prohibited.*

---

* Constituzioni dell' Accademia Reale :—

4. ' Si prohibisce di portar Composizioni satiriche contro chi si sia, né sarà lecito trattar simili materie in publico, nè in segreto.

11. ' Di quest' Accademia si bandiscono tutte le adulatione e lodi toccanti la Regina.

28. ' In quest' Accademia si studi la purità, la gravità, e la maestà della lingua Toscana. S'imitino per quanto si può i maestri della vera eloquenza de' secoli d'Augusto, e di Leone X, poiche negli autori di quei tempi, si trova l'idea d'una perfetta e nobil eloquenza, e però si dia il bando allo stile moderno, turgido ed ampolloso, ai traslati, metafore, figure, &c., dalle quali bisogna astenersi per quanto sarà possibile, o almeno adroprarle con gran discrezione e giudizio.'

Sbozzo dell' Accademia Clementina :—

1. 'L'instituto dell' Accademia sarà il raggionare sopra tutte le materie utili, dilettevoli, erudite e curiose, che possono cadere sotto l'intelletto humano, e che siano degne d'esser discorse in una udienza regia.

Although Christina's revenues were now always in arrear, she contrived to increase her library and her picture gallery. Her support of learned men was as generous as ever, and it was given with such delicacy as greatly enhanced its value. She renewed her intimacy with Holsteinius, who assisted her to arrange her books and manuscripts, although she took a personal and active part herself in the management of her library. Unlike Vossius and her French courtiers, Holsteinius not only stole none of her books, but he proved that his regard and admiration for her were real and unaffected.

At his death, when Christina's generosity could no longer serve him, he left her a considerable number of his own valuable manuscripts.

One of the members of her Academy was the Archbishop Angelo della Noce. He was a man of great taste and learning, but was unfortunately very poor. Christina made him a regular allow-

---

4. 'Tutt' i discorsi si saranno in lingua Italiana, ciascheduno studi d'esser nel suo discorso chiaro, puro, e breve più che sia possibile, procurino d'esser erudite senza pedanteria, ed elo-quenti senza affettazione, in che si dovrà far gran studio.

7. 'Sia bandita dall' Accademia ogni sorta d'adulazione, o Panegirici, e sopra tutto non si parla mai della Regina.'

ance, and gave him the use of one of her carriages.

He was at one time in great pecuniary difficulty. As soon as the Queen heard of it she sent him two hundred ducats, accompanied by the following note :—

" I send you two hundred ducats, which bear no proportion either to your merit, or to my desire to serve you. The shame I feel at sending you such a paltry present must be your revenge.

" Do not mention a word about it to any one, or you will offend me mortally."*

Pallavicini was one of her most enthusiastic admirers. He wrote a work, " On the Great Acquisition the Roman Catholic Church had made in Christina," but his book was never printed, as it was said to contain no less than fifty-four heresies.

Menzini also belonged to her academy. His poems are still esteemed, and he also was indebted to Christina's generosity.

The Italians were not generally wanting in gratitude, and Menzini did his best to celebrate the fame of his patroness.

* Archenholtz. Tome II., p. 140.

Alessandro Guidi held a high place among the later Italian poets, and some of his odes are considered equal to any in the language.*

Immediately on his arrival at Rome, he received the most flattering attentions from Christina. She was so pleased with his treatment of a subject which she gave him, that she 'persuaded him to remain at Rome, gave him a regular pension, and induced the Pope to place him in a lucrative situation.

Guidi celebrated her praises in his poems, and showed a noble and generous mind as well as a graceful flow of verse.

When Christina was dying, all her courtiers came into her presence, not so much to see her for the last time, as in the hope of receiving one more mark of her favour. With the generosity which might be called her ruling passion, she sent none of them away without some gift. Guidi alone did not present himself, but remained outside in prayer for his benefactress.

Filicaja was as worthy a character as Guidi, and he wrote equally good poetry.

He wrote some odes which are highly esteemed,.

* Hallam's ' Lit. of Europe.' Vol· III., p. 461.

on the deliverance of Vienna by the brave Sobieski. His Ode to Rome, on the occasion of Christina taking up her residence there, is also considered a fine piece of poetry.

His talents did not bring him wealth, and he had great difficulty in supporting his family. Christina undertook the charge of his two sons, on condition that the father should keep her generosity a secret. The grateful poet sent her a collection of his verses, with which she was highly pleased, and said that they revived the beauties of Petrarch without his faults.

Filicaja asked permission to compose an ode in her praise, but Christina replied, "I should be sorry that you thought I wished you to praise me, and those who gave you such an idea have done me a great wrong. I have not sought it from any one, and I should not like you to lose your great merit of only praising those who deserve it, for my sake. If you wish to please me, do not waste your time and your talents on me. I will not refuse your offer to work for me. Without flattering me or my faults, you will work for me when you compose on any subject poems worthy of yourself."

The ode was nevertheless written, and Christina

expressed her gratification in a letter, where she said, " I will endeavour to make myself more worthy of your glorious labours, and more like the lofty idea which you have given of me."

This was by no means a solitary instance of her unwillingness to receive flattery.

She had said many years before to Holsteinius, —" I should be offended at what you have said about me if I did not consider you have done yourself more wrong than you have done me, when you endeavoured to pass me off as a scholar. My ignorance will continually contradict you, and I shall be sorry to see you punished for your high opinion of me. You can only excuse yourself by admitting that you have flattered me. What advantage is it for you to have studied the ancient philosophers so carefully, unless you learn from their writings to instruct princes, instead of to flatter them ?"

In May, 1679, she wrote to M. Le Court,— " Your letter expresses sentiments of zeal and affection which cannot but be agreeable to me, although I would have you speak as a philosopher who censures rather than as a courtier who flatters."

In a subsequent letter to the same person she said, " I must forgive your flatteries, for I see that you are incorrigible, and that it is no use quarrelling with you about them.

" I see another fault in you; that you are insincere. You say that you know flattery displeases me. If that was true, would you give it me by handsful as you do?

" You see you are caught, and convicted of a fault which you must correct. . . . . .

" When one has passed fifty years of age, it is too late to accomplish anything . . . . .

" I am sorry that I have profited so little by the incense formerly paid to my rank ; for I think that flattery, which is the poison of princes, might be their best medicine, if they knew how to use it properly. It is too late for me, so you should spare the friends that you cannot improve."

After this she wrote to Francis Lemene, a member of her Academy,—

" I return your dedication, which would be very fine if it were not written for me.

" Some may say that your flattery pleases me, but I will confess that you would have pleased me much more if you had praised me less. I fear that your partiality may injure me more than you imagine. If all comparisons are odious, what must a comparison be between me and Alexander the Great?"

Christina had always had a taste for mathematics, and at Rome she paid particular attention to that science. She passed many hours with Cassini, when he was making his observations.

It was in the Chigi palace, and in her presence, that he discovered a comet. He traced on the celestial globe the course it would take, and Christina carefully verified the correctness of his hypothesis. She also took great interest in the studies of Borelli. This eminent mathematician widened the sphere of knowledge by using one science to elucidate another.

In his treatise, "De motu Animalium," he applied mathematical principles to anatomy with clearness and ingenuity.

The reign of Clement IX. has been called the golden age of Rome. Unfortunately it only lasted two years, as he died in 1669, and it is said that, his grief at the conquest of Candia by the Turks was fatal to him.

Cardinal Altieri, who then succeeded him as

Clement X., partook in a considerable degree of his mild and amiable disposition.

He was succeeded by a Pontiff of a very different character. Innocent XI. was stern and severe, and Christina soon had some serious disputes with him. She, however, did him good service in the affair of Molinos, and it was in a great measure through her exertions that peace was restored to the Roman Church.

It was about this time that Christina's domains in Pomerania were in the most critical state, on account of the war between Sweden and Brandenburg.

This war was brought about by the corruption of the faction which ruled Sweden, and chiefly by Magnus de la Gardie.

During the minority of Charles XI. the nobility became even more powerful than they had been under Christina.

We shall see the disgrace and ruin which their conduct brought upon Sweden. We shall see their unscrupulous schemes stripped of the pretence of patriotism, and no longer adorned by the glitter of success. The vices of an aristocratic rule, a selfish and oppressive spirit, will appear unredeemed by the steadfastness of purpose and the sense of honour which often characterise that form of government. We shall especially remark that Christina's two bitterest enemies, noblemen of the very highest rank, De la Gardie and Brahe, acquired a dishonourable pre-eminence in taking gifts from a foreign government, and that they directed the policy and arms of their country to promote the objects of Louis XIV., by whom they were bribed.

The nobles resolved to avoid the mistake they had made in the education of Christina, and to profit by the natural idleness of the young King to keep the power in their own hands.

The Queen Dowager was a weak and ignorant woman. She was easily led to adopt the system of the Regents, without perceiving their object. She constantly said, " Do not contradict my son : the great thing is to keep him in good health : my brothers never learned anything, and yet they make very good princes."

Charles was idle, but not indolent, and the Regents forgot that public affairs themselves educate a man of good natural ability.

When Charles awoke to the sense of his own deficiencies he soon took steps to remedy them,

and he said of himself, " I learned those things
while carrying on war, which people usually forget
under such circumstances." The disasters which
were caused by the bad advice of the Senate, were
retrieved by his own ability; and the nobles, who
had expected to render Charles their puppet, received from him the heaviest blow that had ever
befallen the Swedish aristocracy.

During Charles's minority, the Senate was
divided into two factions. Bonde, Oxenstiern, and
Fleming wished for peace and retrenchment; but
the other party, headed by De la Gardie, Stenbock,
and Wrangel, was the most powerful.

De la Gardie wished for war because he shared
largely in the grants which the Regents made to
themselves after any success, and he was also
anxious to get rid of Wrangel, who was his most
powerful rival.

When a fresh war was proposed, Bonde earnestly
opposed it. He said that Sweden was weakened
and exhausted, and that peace was essential for
her restoration. Even if a fresh war was successful, all Europe would consider Sweden a nation of
pirates and robbers, and would form a league
against her. The boasted successes were of little

use; a few individuals were enriched, but the country in general was impoverished and depopulated. The conquests did not produce so much as they cost to win and to maintain.

These arguments did not prevent the commencement of an aggressive war against Bremen in 1666, but Holland, Brandenburg, Denmark, and Austria united to protect Bremen, and Sweden was obliged to make peace, with no other result than an expense of two million rix-dollars. Even then De la Gardie opposed the disbanding of the troops, on the ground that some other employment might presently be found for them.

In 1668 De la Gardie's power was somewhat diminished, and notwithstanding, his opposition, Sweden entered into the triple alliance with England and Holland for the purpose of restraining Louis XIV.

Our old acquaintance, Van Beunigen, was as active against Louis as he had been against Charles Gustavus. When Louis attacked Holland, his flatterers compared him to the rising-sun.

The Dutch struck a medal, in which Van Beunigen was represented as Joshua commanding the sun to stand still.

The triple alliance did not last long. The governments of England and of Sweden were equally corrupt, and Louis XIV. bribed them to attack Holland, which they were pledged to defend.

The English nation was not a party to this perfidy. Notwithstanding their old jealousy of the Dutch, the English did not wish to be the tools of French ambition. They declared that in the sea-fights with the Dutch they were both made gladiators for French spectators. Dutch sailors said that the French hired the English to fight for them, and only looked on themselves to see that the money was earned. The parliament echoed the voice of the people in accents which reminded Charles II. how terrible that assembly might again become if too much provoked. He consented unwillingly to end a war which he had undertaken from no motives of policy, but only to acquire French gold for the gratification of his private pleasures.

Louis also endeavoured to bribe the great Elector of Brandenburg; but the character and abilities of this prince were too lofty for him to fall into the condition of a vassal or a tool.

He would not even promise to remain neutral, and Louis then determined to employ the arms of Sweden against him.

Seldom have more disgraceful negotiations been carried on than those in which the Swedish Senate now engaged.

They had no cause of quarrel with Brandenburg. No principle of sound policy recommended such a war.

It was a mere matter of bargain. Louis and the Swedish nobles chaffered, disputed, and tried to cheat each other about the price of blood.

De la Gardie hesitated to the last. He saw that the war was impolitic, and that it might be disastrous; but what affected him most was the chance that he might be called to account if anything went wrong.

When a government is hired to perform acts of violence and injustice, it is an easy step for individual members of that government to accept separate bribes.

De la Gardie's timidity was overcome at last by a present of 30,000 dollars.*

Feuquière, the French ambassador at Stock-

* Fryxell. P. 39.

holm, distributed gratifications in the most delicate way among the Swedish nobles. He gave magnificent banquets at the commencement of the year, and the bribes were called new year's gifts.

Wrangel's and De la Gardie's wives received splendid diamonds and costly dresses.

The proud and aristocratic Brahe valued his hitherto unsullied honour at 12,000 dollars.*

The nobles in opposition, Bjelke, Oxenstiern, and Gripenhjelm, were bribed by Spain, but the Spanish Court was poor.

Some jewels were sent and accepted, but without the mixture of hard cash that the Swedish nobles loved.

The party that was paid the highest, was the most zealous, and it was determined to send an army to Germany.

The Swedish Council tried hard to get some money in advance, but on this point Feuquière was inexorable, and the young King himself was refused when he asked for a small instalment, and pledged his royal word that the troops should be sent.

Feuquière was perfectly right, for at the last

* Fryxell. Femtonde Delen. P. 30.

moment De la Gardie proposed to the King to get what money they could from France, and then, instead of sending the troops to Germany, to make a sudden attack upon the Danes.

Charles approved of the plan, and it did not fail from any remorse on his part, or on that of his minister. One of the Council, Dulle Banaren, (the stupid Banér,) accidentally revealed the plot, and thus warned France and Denmark of the intended perfidy.*

Wrangel arrived at last in Brandenburg, with 16,000 men, but when there he received the most contradictory orders from De la Gardie. At one time he was told to commence active operations, and at another time ordered to remain quiet, as if in a neutral, rather than a hostile country.

It was said the vacillation of the Swedish Government was so extreme, that in six days Wrangel received six opposite orders.

When the Swedish army entered Brandenburg, the Elector was engaging a French army upon the Rhine, and his own country was quite defenceless against so unexpected an attack; but Frederick

* Rådsprot, d. 26 Oct., 1674. Riksregistratur, Bref till K. G. Wrangel, d. 24 Oct., 1674.

William's courage and sagacity did not desert him. He opposed stratagem to perfidy, until he was able to meet force with force, and he dissembled his resentment until he could make it felt. The first contest was one of diplomacy, and in that the Swedes were outwitted. They believed that the Elector was overawed by their power, because that prudent prince appeared anxious for peace and reconciliation.

By this means he gained time, and saved his country from being ravaged by a hostile army.

The Swedish Senate and Council were thoroughly perplexed. They dispatched orders to Wrangel on the 14th of January, to abstain from any act of hostility.

Two days later he was ordered to seize at once upon four strong places in Brandenburg.*

Ten days after this he was told to exercise his own discretion as to commencing or delaying the attack.†

Frederick William acted steadily and swiftly, without hesitation or delay. He opened active

* Riksregistratur, Bref till K. G. Wrangel. d. 16 Jan. 1675.

† Riksregistratur, Bref till K. G. Wrangel. d. 26 Jan 1675.

negotiations with Holland, Denmark, Austria, and England, and he went himself to the Hague, which was then the centre of opposition to France.

Sweden had an ambassador at the Hague, who had hitherto ably maintained the interests of his country, but from the time that Fredrick William arrived there, all Ehrensten's efforts were fruitless.*

Holland, Denmark, and Austria agreed to declare war upon Sweden, and as soon as the Elector had gained these allies, he began to show what he could do for himself. He rejoined his army, and marched swiftly and secretly to the relief of his country.

He reached Magdeburg on the 11th of June, and rested his troops there two days, during which time the gates were kept closed, in order that no information might reach the Swedes, who were separated into three divisions, and were quite unaware of their enemy's approach.

Seven thousand of the best Prussian troops marched all the night of the 13th, and all the following day, through a heavy rain, to Ratenau.

So accurately had everything been timed, that

* 'Men frȧn det ögonblick Fredrik Wilhelm kom dit, blefvo alla Ehrensteen's bemödanden fȧfȧnga.' Fryxell, 15. Delen. P.54

a nobleman named Baron Brist, had, by the Elector's order, invited the chief officers of the Swedish garrison to a grand banquet on the night of the 14th, in order the more effectually to put them off their guard.

About daylight on the morning of the 15th, when the Swedish commanders were all drunk, the Elector's troops attacked Ratenau. Although almost without officers, the Swedish veterans made a defence worthy of their reputation, but in an hour and a half they were all killed or made prisoners.

The Swedes thought they had secured all the passes over the Revel, but by his exploit at Ratenau the Elector not only secured the passage of the river, but also interposed his own army between two divisions of the Swedes. He attacked the largest division with so much skill, that it was obliged to retreat before an inferior force.

The Prince of Hesse-Homburg followed the Swedes with 1,500 light cavalry, and, although frequently repulsed, continually renewed his attacks, and harassed the enemy so effectually that the Elector was able to catch them up at Fehr-Bellin.

In the battle which ensued the Elector dis-

played as much daring courage as he had previously shown cool sagacity. The end of all his
schemes had been to place himself sword in hand
before the invaders of his country. Both sides
fought with great determination, and the Swedish
Life Guards preferred being cut to pieces to
yielding.

The Elector fought like a common soldier, or
rather as few common soldiers could be expected
to fight : at one time he had penetrated so far
among the enemy that he was only rescued by the
most desperate exertions of his own men.

The Swedes were defeated, and although they
retired in good order, they could no longer make
head against the increasing forces of Brandenburg.

Frederick William was not satisfied with driving
the enemy out of his own country. With the
assistance of the Danes he conquered the whole of
Swedish Pomerania, although, by the intervention
of France, it was afterwards restored to Sweden.

When Pomerania became the seat of war Christina's revenues were still more diminished, although
the Elector desired that her domains should not
be molested, and gave a safeguard for that purpose. When hostile armies were contending it

was impossible that this safeguard should be strictly observed, and as it turned out, it was rather a compliment than a benefit to Christina.

Her circumstances for some time were seriously straitened, as will appear from extracts of her letters. She wrote to Gyllenstiern in August, 1676, —" I rested my hopes upon the King's promises, that before this time I should receive my subsidy of 30,000 dollars, and 60,000 more in compensation for my revenues, which were used for the public service in the present emergency."

Shortly afterwards, addressing the same nobleman, she said, " I beg you to be more assiduous in my affairs, and to recollect that, whilst you gentlemen ' are drinking my health in the country, my affairs are neglected at Stockholm, and I am in danger of starving at Rome. Texeira receives no money. I hear nothing of my revenues. I receive no money from any quarter. What is to be done ? No one pays me, but every one expects me to pay them.

" I wish you would either teach me the secret how to live without money, or else manage my affairs better."*

* Archenholtz, Tome II., p 167.

The fortunes of Sweden seemed desperate, when, after her expulsion from Germany, her own territory was invaded by superior forces, and her navy was swept from the sea by Juel and Van Tromp. She was saved by the genius and heroism of the young King at the great battle of Lund, a battle of which a warlike nation might be justly proud. The tide of disaster was now stemmed, and the Swedes met with no more considerable reverses by land, except one, where Magnus de la Gardie was intrusted with a division. He was defeated with the loss of his baggage and artillery, and forfeited for ever the favour of the King. The once rich and powerful nobleman died in poverty and disgrace, and Christina was at last revenged.

Soon after the peace of Nimeguen, Charles XI. married Ulrica Eleanora, the sister of the King of Denmark. This amiable Princess had been engaged to him before the war broke out, and she proved her good-will to the nation with which she was about to become connected, by her kindness to the Swedish prisoners. In order to alleviate their distresses she more than once sold her jewels.

Charles had won the heart of his people in the

most accessible point, their love of military glory; and he was now in a position to shake off the bondage in which the nobles had kept their sovereigns.

A long series of wrongs, beginning from the time of Christina's minority, had to be redressed, which required the strong hand and the stern will of the victorious monarch.

In the Diet of 1680, Charles had no difficulty in gaining the clergy, citizens, and peasants, for they all had abundant cause to complain of the nobles. The minor nobles also had suffered from the same oppression, and Charles gained more votes in the Chamber of Peers by creating several of his Generals Barons. Although Charles, like Christina, had given an indemnity to the Regents, less scrupulous than she was, he reversed this guarantee, and condemned them to refund all the sums to which they had helped themselves. Wrangel's heirs were sentenced to pay 250,000 dollars, De la Gardie 110,000, Stenbock 100,000, and Brahe 430,000.

This, however, was only a part of what the nobles had to refund, for at the same time Charles resumed all the grants that had been made to them since the time of Gustavus Adolphus. A complete revolution was effected. The Senators were no longer styled an independent order, but were called the King's Senators, and were allowed to give no opinion without the King's command.

These changes were carried out so relentlessly that many families were reduced from opulence to actual poverty. The amiable Queen ventured to intercede in some cases which were particularly hard, but Charles was determined to have no half-measures with the nobles. He knew that he had offended them past all forgiveness, and he was determined to make their resentment impotent. He checked the Queen's interference with very little ceremony.

"Madam," he said, "we took you to give us children, and not to give us advice."

Christina must have been more than human if she had not felt some satisfaction at the humiliation of the order by whom she had been robbed, insulted, and traduced; but she was too generous to strike the fallen, and it does not appear that any reproaches from her ever added to their distress.

As time passed on, Christina became accustomed to view public affairs as a spectator and a critic, although she was to the last most tenacious of her privileges.

A serious and religious spirit appears in her letter to the Count Wasenau, which her writings did not often exhibit. She detested anything that bore the slightest appearance of hypocrisy, and seldom introduced religious subjects in her letters. For this reason there is the more cause to believe that she expressed her genuine sentiments to Wasenau.

Count Wasenau was a natural son of Uladislaus of Poland, and was consequently Christina's cousin.

John Casimir had treated him kindly, but never acknowledged him as a relation. After the abdication of John Casimir, Wasenau went to Rome, where Christina at once received him as a cousin, and gave him an appointment in her Court. She also sent him on a mission to Sweden, where he served her with fidelity. There was nothing very remarkable about Wasenau, but his character was upright and honourable, and his manners were refined and distinguished.

Christina felt considerable anxiety about his prospects in case of her death. She left him a small pension, which it does not appear that he ever received, as on the loss of his benefactress he was reduced to poverty.

Cardinal Albani procured him an office in the Papal Court, and on his death, at the age of seventy-five, erected a monument to "his honourable and pious friend."

When Christina felt this anxiety about providing for him, she wrote Wasenau the following interesting letter :—

"The state of your affairs, and of my own, lead me to give you advice which will perhaps surprise you.

"But if you reflect seriously, you will be convinced that it is my kindness, or rather the kindness of God, towards you, which leads me to persuade you to leave the Court and the gay world as soon as possible.

"It seems to me that your best course would be to retire either to Monte-Cassino or to Vall'Ombrosa, either of which are beautiful places, and to consecrate the rest of your days to the service of God, by taking the vows. You are happy to be able

to do so, and I envy your state, which makes such
a noble resolution practicable for you. There is
nothing so great, so glorious, or so beautiful, as to
dedicate oneself without reserve to God. It will
be well for you if you embrace this opportunity
with joy and with courage.

" You have nothing to hope for in the world or at
the Court; you are unfortunate in not having the
means to support your birth. I am not able to
make your fortune; I am more unfortunate than
you, because I am greater, and because I am not
able to adopt a similar resolution. There is nothing for you nor for me to hope for, and one is
happiest when one does not expect or hope for anything in this world. Man is made for something
greater, and the world has nothing which can
sstisfy him.

" If you could become a monarch, and be surrounded with glory and pleasure, you would not be
more satisfied than you are at present.

" I speak from experience, you would not be
more satisfied ; on the contrary, you would have
troubles and annoyances which are now unknown
to you, and which are worse than those that you
have experienced. . . . If you are convinced

of this truth, you will joyfully enter the harbour which God's providence opens, to save you from shipwreck. Still, before you determine, examine your own heart well. Do not trust in yourself, but trust in God, and if you are convinced of your vocation, leave the world at once; leave it as you would do a burning house. Give bravely the little that you have to God, and do not fear to lose by it; He will repay you with usury; for God is so good that He rewards us, although we only give Him what is already His own.

"What glory and pleasure to serve so good a master, and how happy I am to have given up so much for Him! This satisfaction is worth more than the empire of the world.

"Believe me, it is the best policy, because, sooner or later, one must die. If, however, you desire to enter any profession, I do not oppose it. Follow your own inclination, and pray God to lead you to do what is most to His glory, and to your own happiness." . . .

One of the noblest traits in Christina's character was her hatred of bigotry, and her courage in expressing that hatred. Converts are generally very reluctant to censure any extravagance in the religion of their adoption. They generally think it necessary to prove their sincerity by siding with the most extreme party. Christina did not hesitate to express her abhorrence of the religious persecutions which Louis XIV. perpetrated, with a piety as ruthless as his ambition. She wrote the following letter to the Chevalier Terlon, on the subject of the infamous Dragonades:—

"As you wish to know my opinions of the pretended extirpation of heresy in France, I am very glad to communicate them to you, and as I neither fear nor flatter any one, I will tell you plainly that I have no great faith in the success of this design, nor can I consider it advantageous to our holy religion; on the contrary, I foresee the prejudice which it will everywhere raise against us.

"Between ourselves—Are you satisfied of the sincerity of these new converts?

"I wish that they may obey God and their King without dissimulation, but I dread their obstinacy, and would not be responsible for the sacrileges committed by Catholics under the coercion of missionaries who treat our holy mysteries in so reckless a manner.

"Soldiers are strange apostles, and I believe

them more apt to kill, to steal, and to violate, than
to persuade.   In fact, trustworthy accounts inform
us that they do perform their mission very much
in this way.   I commiserate the people abandoned
to their discretion; I pity so many ruined families, so many honest people reduced to beggary;
and I cannot contemplate what is now going on in
France without grief.

" I lament that these unfortunate people are in
error; but it appears to me that they are deserving
of pity rather than of hatred.

" I would not for the whole world either share
in their error, or be the author of their present
misery.   I consider France like a sick person,
whose arms and legs are cut off to remedy a disease, which a little patience and kindness would
have entirely cured. I fear that the disease will be
aggravated, and will become incurable.

" Nothing is more laudable than the desire to
convert heretics and infidels, but the manner of
accomplishing it is strange; and since our Lord
did not employ such means to convert the world,
they cannot be the most desirable means.

" I cannot understand such zeal; and such
policy passes my comprehension.   I am very glad

that I cannot understand it . . . .
I have sufficient love for France to lament the
desolation of so beautiful a country.

"I hope that I may be mistaken, and that
everything may turn out to the glory of God, and
of the King your master.

"Rome, 2nd Feby., 1686."

The expression of these sentiments did not altogether please the French, and Christina was
censured by some who had not even the excuse of
religious enthusiasm. Bayle, whose sceptical
opinions are well known, was inconsistent enough
to blame her for this letter, and to call it a rem-
nant of Protestantism. Christina remonstrated
warmly at this accusation, and after some correspondence on the subject, Bayle apologised. The
Queen received his excuses very graciously. She
said, " You express so much regret, that I have
resolved to show you by this letter that I forgive
you with all my heart. What chiefly offended me
was the accusation of Protestantism, for I am
very sensitive on that point. I will not, however,
let you get off so easily as you expect; I will
impose a penance, which is that you shall send me all

* Archenholtz, Tome II. P. 167.

the good scientific books you can find, whether in Latin, French, Spanish, or Italian. Send me your journal also, and I will pay all expenses."

The free-thinkers were not always very candid, and many of them acted on the maxim which one of them uttered, " To think whatever one pleased, but to do whatever other people did."*

There was perhaps more bigotry in France, and more superstition in Italy; but the superstition was less cruel and aggressive than the bigotry.

Learned men in Italy could venture sometimes to throw a little ridicule on superstition, which was chiefly confined to the ignorant; but in France bigotry was seated in the highest place, and has seldom been more remorseless.†

Although Christina was jealous of her reputa-

* It was said of Cremonini, Professor of Philosophy at Padua, 'Nihil habebat pietatis et tamen pius haberi volebat. Une de ses maximes etait. Intus ut libet; foris ut moris est.' —Naudeana, p. 56. Amsterdam, 1703.

† ' Caporali was Secretary to a Cardinal at Rome. He was always poor and unfortunate. He said that if chance had made him a hatter, God would have made men without heads.' —Naudeana, p. 123.—'Naudé, ridiculing the quarrels between the citizens of Imola, and their neighbours at Brisiguelle, says that the latter altered the words in the Mass, " qui immolatus est pro nobis," and substituted, " qui Brisiguellatus est pro nobis." ' P. 72.

tion for orthodoxy, she was never betrayed into any intolerance; and about this time she had the courage to attempt, and the power to accomplish, the rescue of two gentlemen from the jaws of the Spanish Inquisition.

CHAPTER VI.

CHRISTINA had lived quietly for some years at
Rome, when she was again roused to politi ca

affairs by the intelligence that Charles XI. had received severe injuries by a fall from his horse, and that it was doubtful whether he would recover. She was afraid that her revenues might be endangered by any change of Government, and she wrote to Olivecrantz, the governor of her domains, desiring him to call attention to her claims, in case the family of Charles Gustavus should become extinct.

The practice of surgery had, however, improved in Sweden, and a broken leg was no longer likely to lead to fatal results.

Charles soon recovered from his accident, and Christina's anxiety was set at rest a few months afterwards by the birth of a prince, who became so famous as Charles XII.

By a singular coincidence, a report was circulated about the same time, in Sweden, of Christina's death.

As soon as she heard of it, she wrote one of her characteristic letters to Olivecrantz :—

" Regarding the report of my death I am not surprised at it ; there are many people who desire it. It is natural they should sometimes indulge in flattering illusions.

"My death will happen when God pleases, but I am not so far advanced in grace as to wish for it. I am in perfect health and strength, and although that is no security against death, yet, judging from appearances, many people who little expect it, will die before me. I assure you that I await death with tranquillity.

"Whenever it pleases God to terminate my life, they will be informed of it in Sweden, and have the satisfaction of learning it in a way which cannot be doubted. I have friends and attendants who will perform this office for me.

"Believe nothing you hear until it reaches you in this authentic manner, and above all let me assure you that neither fear nor interest will ever kill me. If there were no other cause of death than these, I should be immortal."

The events which took place in Hungary showed that Christina's apprehension of the Turks was not unfounded. Fortunately for the Empire, Leopold had made an alliance with Poland, and the heroic Sobieski, with 70,000 men, totally defeated the immense invading army, amounting to 300,000. Christina expressed the most cordial admiration of the Polish King. She said:—

" Your Majesty has displayed to the world a great and noble spectacle by the deliverance of Vienna, and the memory of it should be immortalized in the annals of Christianity.

" The gratitude which is due to you is as universal as it is profound, but it is also the duty of everyone to record his own individual joy.

" I wish that I could express my sentiments in a manner worthy of the occasion, and I feel sure you will be persuaded that no one does more justice than myself to your extraordinary merit. I may even boast of feeling more than any one the value and importance of your Majesty's glorious victory over the Emperor of Asia, because I was more penetrated than anyone with our danger, and with the desolation and ruin which threatened us. Heaven has employed your valour to save us, and, next to God, the other Princes owe the preservation of their States to you.

" For myself, although I no longer reign, I owe you the same obligation as these other Sovereigns, for I owe to you the preservation of my royal independence, and the repose which I prefer to any kingdom.

" I must still confess my ingratitude to so great

a King as your Majesty, because I feel envy, a sen-
timent all the more painful to me because I have
never before experienced it. No living being has
hitherto excited envy in my heart; you alone
have subjected me to a feeling of which I believed
myself incapable. This does not interfere with
the esteem and admiration which you so well
deserve. I do not envy you your kingdom, your
treasures, or the trophies of your valour. I envy
your dangers and fatigues, the title of the Champion of Christianity, and the satisfaction of restor-
ing liberty to those (both friends and enemies)
who are released from slavery by your Majesty's
orders.

"The envy which I feel is so glorious to your
Majesty, that I do not desire to be released from
it, and I hope your Majesty will forgive me. May
God, who is the source of all glory and greatness,
reward your Majesty in this world and in
eternity!"

A very injurious custom prevailed at Rome with
regard to the foreign ambassadors. Not only
were they and their suites exempt from the opera-
tion of the laws, but this immunity extended to
a certain distance from their residences. Any out-

law or criminal who took refuge in these districts was safe from all pursuit. We know by tradition what an intolerable evil one sanctuary of this sort was in London, and may form some idea of the confusion which must have arisen when a dozen such refuges were tolerated in Rome.

Innocent XI. resolved to restrict this privilege to the palaces of the ambassadors.

Christina saw at once the justice of this alteration, and before any positive steps were taken by the Pope, she set the example of resigning so unreasonable a power. She wrote to him :—

" In the wish of forwarding the just intentions of your Holiness, I propose to resign for ever a right which I have hitherto possessed through your indulgence and that of your predecessors. I only reserve this right so far as regards people in my own service. I confess that I only offer you what is already your own, but neither can we offer to God anything that is not already His ; yet in His infinite goodness He not only accepts, but rewards such offerings."

The Pope did not think it incumbent on him to imitate this goodness, and he received Christina's concession rather ungraciously.

The Emperor and the King of Spain conformed to the Pope's wishes, but Louis XIV. insisted on maintaining his prerogative. He said, with reference to the other monarchs, that he was accustomed to set examples, and not to follow them, and that the many services rendered by France might well establish her claim to some exclusive privilege.

The Pope did not admit the justice of this argument, and he excommunicated the French ambassador.

As Innocent did not hesitate even to offend the powerful King of France, it was not likely he would have much consideration for Christina, and the way in which she was treated was so contrary to the custom of the time, that she had some cause to think herself outraged. The police arrested an obscure individual in one of the churches at Rome ; the man escaped from their hands, and took refuge in Christina's stables, but the police had so little discretion in carrying out their duty, that they seized the man again even within the precincts of her palace.

Christina with some reason considered this an affront to herself, and she ordered her captain of the guards to release the man.* The mob was delighted at the high-handed assertion of a privilege which might become useful to any member of it, and the people shouted " Viva la Regina !"

The Papal authorities took a different view of the matter, and the treasurer published a violent order, which condemned Christina's officer and soldiers to death. She wrote to the treasurer :—

" In your tribunal, you and your master call dishonouring yourselves, doing justice. I pity you very much, but I shall pity you still more when you become cardinal.

" In the meantime I give you my word that those whom you have condemned to death shall (God willing) live a little longer, and if they die any other than a natural death, they shall not die alone."

Christina then assembled her household, and offered to release any one who did not wish to share in her danger, but they all declared with emotion that they would shed their blood for her.

She then had the audacity to brave the Pope by

* Relation veritable de la demission que la Reine de Suéde fit de son quartier a Rome, le 3 Avril, 1687. Rome, 1687.

going to the church of the Jesuits, accompanied by the whole of her household in military order.

As any violence might have gained her the support of France, the Pope began to temporize a little, and sent Christina a present of some véry rare fruits. She received the compliment ungraciously enough, and said, " He need not expect to put me to sleep, for I will be on my guard."

Innocent replied by a sarcasm that was none the less bitter, that it consisted of only two words, " E donna."

Never since the time of Falstaff's hostess was a similar provocation so warmly received, and as she expressed her indignation without reserve, the Pope thought he would punish her further, although, in fact, he did not annoy her nearly so much by his acts as he had done by his satire.

The pension of 12,000 dollars which had been granted to her by Alexander VII., and continued by the succeeding pontiffs, was now withdrawn. The announcement was made to her by Azzolini, and she sent the following answer :—

" I assure you that you have given me the most agreeable news in the world. God, who knows my heart, knows that I tell the truth. The pension which the Pope gave me was the one blot of my life, and I received it from God as the greatest humiliation to which He could put my pride. I trust that I have found favour with Him, now that He removes this trial in a way so glorious for me. . . . . .

" I beg you to convey my thanks to Cardinal Cibo, and to the Pope, for relieving me from this obligation . . . . . ."

When Christina's uncomfortable position at Rome became known, the Elector of Brandenburg offered her an asylum in his dominions, and he sent his chamberlain, Dobrinsky, to make the communication to her. The Queen was gratified at this consideration of her old lover, and would have availed herself of it if the Pope had proceeded to extremities. Christina, however, was not destined to wander any further, and the time was near at hand when she would want no support from Pope or Prince.

One of the last objects she had at heart was to prevent Sweden from engaging in another war at the instigation of France.

Louis XIV. invaded the empire again in 1688, but Charles XI. understood the interests of his

country better than the Regents had done, and
kept resolutely aloof from the war. The result of
his good sense was that Sweden continued to increase in prosperity and wealth, and when peace
was made some years later, he held the dignified
position of arbitrator.

James II. of England, like all the House of Stuart,
leaned towards a French alliance, but he was unable to carry out his intention, for his sceptre was
even now about to pass into the hand of the most
irreconcilable enemy of Louis XIV.

Christina's opinions of the proper Swedish policy,
and of the Prince of Orange, are expressed in a
letter to Olivecrantz.

" I am persuaded that the wisest course for Sweden, is to remain neutral, and I am most impatient
to know what she will do. France is continually
advancing, and does what she pleases, without meeting any resistance. The English affairs are in a
sad state. The bigotry of the Jesuits and monks
has ruined the King, and I predicted his ruin long
ago. If the Prince of Orange succeeds in his enterprise, as I believe he will, England and Holland
will be a formidable power when united under the
same head, and that such a head as the Prince. I

am very much deceived if he does not check France, and make her repent the cruel persecution of the Huguenots.—Dec. 4, 1688."

A few days later, she wrote, "If you had heard my predictions, the last three years, of which all Rome is witness, you would confess that I understand astrology better than the English, and that terrestial astrology is better than celestial.

"Bigotry, the advice of Jesuits, monks, and priests infallibly ruin those who are governed by them.

"I will make you another prophesy, which is, that England and Holland united will make all Europe tremble, and will impose laws both by sea and by land. Remember my words."*

As soon as her prognostications were verified, and William III. was seated on the throne of England, Christina wrote to intercede with him on behalf of the English Catholics. "That little flock," she said, "will not interfere with your affairs; they will be too happy to live quietly. Their weakness leaves you nothing to fear from them: everything is subject to you; every one praises your fortune and your glory.

"I am only sorry your glory causes unhappiness

* Archenholtz. Tome II., p. 297.

to others. Do not be offended, for I do not the less esteem and admire you."

About six months before her death Christina lost a faithful and useful servant in the Marquis del Monte. His son was at the time in Sweden, where the Queen had sent him about the proposed exchange of Bremen for her domains in Pomerania.

Her letter to the young man, in which she announced his father's death, is full of sympathy and kindness. Although unaware that her own death would follow so soon, her letter is remarkable for its piety and resignation:—

" I am inconsolable, Marquis, at the loss we have sustained in your father, who as I trust surely is now in eternal glory.

" I share fully in your just sorrow, but we must submit to the Divine will. All that I can do is to assure you that your father has bequeathed to me all his affection for you. . . . . . I have lost so faithful and so able a servant, that my heart bleeds at the thought.

"God, who alone can reward his merit and virtue, has seen my inability to repay the honourable and faithful services he rendered me, and has taken him away to reward him for me.

"I cannot answer your letter, or give you any orders. The wound I have received is too recent.

"Yesterday your father was in as perfect health as a young man like yourself might be; he was with me until three o'clock, and went away very happy. He was taken ill this morning, and at sunset he was dead. What are we? Dust, ashes, nothing! God have mercy upon us, and give us grace to live and die in His favour; everything else is but vanity. . . . . We must all disappear like shadows. Life is but a dream, and it vanishes like lightning: we are all hurrying to eternity; God grant in His mercy that we may reach it happily!"

In February, 1689, Christina had a dangerous attack of erysipelas and fever. She then received the Sacrament, and the Pope sent Cardinal Attaboni to convey to her his benediction. To the surprise of every one, and to her own surprise, she recovered. She wrote to Olivecrantz:—" God has been pleased to snatch me unexpectedly from the arms of death. I was already prepared for that last journey which I thought at hand. God's mercy, combined with nature and art, has restored me to health."

Two months later she had a relapse, but this

time the erysipelas was suppressed, and it soon appeared that the case was hopeless.

The dying Queen sent to beg the Pope's forgiveness for the offence she had given him, and to bespeak his good-will towards her servants.

The Pope sent her absolution, and promised to visit her himself, but before he came she expired so easily and quietly that her attendants could hardly distinguish the sleep of death from the sleep of exhaustion.*

She died on the 19th of April, at the age of sixty-three.

Before her death Christina had conquered one of her weaknesses, the love of display. She expressed a wish that her funeral might be a perfectly plain one, in the Church of the Rotunda, and that the only inscription might be "Vixit Christina annos sexaginta tres."

The Pope, however, determined to give her a public funeral, and a monument in St. Peter's.

The procession was opened by those who were really the chief mourners, the most distinguished learned and literary men. After them came the

* Infermita, Morte, e Funerale della Real Maesta d Cristina Alessandra. Roma, 1689.

religious orders, and the clergy. The Cardinals were dressed in violet, and whatever may have been Innocent's feelings towards Christina during her life, he certainly omitted no mark of respect to her memory.

He followed her too closely to be able to erect any monument to her honour, but Clement XI. raised a memorial of her in St. Peter's; and also struck a medal in remembrance of her.

A contemporary writer says, " And thus the body of Christina Alessandra, Queen of Sweden, remained in the Basilica of St. Peter's; and until the last day will live the fame of this Princess, who was a true example of religion, of generosity, and of the rarest virtue."*

The moral to be drawn from Christina's life is so evident, that it would be useless to dwell on reflections which must present themselves to every reader.

Her abdication was her most fatal mistake.

Rank, wealth, and genius could not atone for the neglect of duty.

The restless activity, which, in its proper sphere,

* Infermita, Morte, e Funerale della Real Maesta di Cristina Alessandra.   Roma, 1689.

might have been a source of pleasure to herself
and of benefit to her people, led to disappointment
and uneasiness when deprived of its legitimate objects.

The bitter attacks which have clouded her fame,
originated chiefly in her disregard of conventional-
ities, with which no rank or station can safely
dispense

Her wit, her generosity, her love of toleration,
and even her piety, furnished weapons against her,
because she offended against small and apparently
unimportant proprieties.

The first article in Christina's will, after the dis-
posal of her body, and the payment for 20,000
masses for her soul, was regarding her debts—she
said, " We desire that our heir shall pay our debts,
if there are any."

She had always shown the greatest anxiety on
this subject, and when, after long delays, she received a large sum of money which was due to her,
the first thing she thought of was her debt to
Texeira. She wrote to Gyllenstiern about him.
"Texeira, as you say, will always have his interest
paid punctually, and he must always have some_
thing towards the liquidation.

" I would rather eat dry bread than not pay my debts. It is no use saying I would rather drink cold water, for I never drink anything else, and should not do so if I had the wealth of Crœsus. You need not be uneasy about Texeira, for I think more of him than of myself. I should be in despair if I were wanting to anyone who had confided in me."

All her servants received legacies, but the bulk of her property was left to Azzolini, " as a mark of affection, esteem, and gratitude."

Bernini's statue of Christ was left to the Pope, and as Azzolini died two months after the Queen, a great part of her library was purchased for the Vatican.

Charles XI. was not mentioned in her will, but his court was put into deep mourning, and he sent a circular to foreign powers, requesting they would pay her the same mark of respect.

It may create some surprise that the writings, or rather fragments, of Christina's own composition do not display more talent.

Her reflections on Alexander and Cæsar are not

* Archenholtz. Tome II. p 166,

without some merit, but that they do not approach
any degree of excellence is sufficiently proved by
the fact that they are never read. Her " maxims,"
or ."thoughts," are occasionally profound, but
often commonplace, and sometimes contradictory.
A few examples will enable the reader to class
them.

" It is with benefits as with seeds : they must be
scattered in profusion, and at hazard."

" The body should be kept in subjection : it
should be treated as a slave, but a slave who
deserves some charity." ·

" Small princes can do a great deal of harm,
but very little good."

" One should seldom pardon those who deserve
to be punished."

" It is the greatest cruelty to spare the guilty."

" The sea resembles great souls: however
agitate the surface may be, the depth is always
calm."

" The good and evil of this world is like those
perspectives which only amuse or deceive at a
distance."

" Men fight duels because they do not understand
true honour."

"One cannot always despise calumny, but one should always despise flattery."

"One should not deceive even an enemy when he confides in us."

"Ignorance is not innocence."

"Luxury does not ruin states; it polishes and enriches them."

"All that is spent in arms and soldiers is economy."

"Great armies are nothing but a collection of weakness."

"Small armies are expensive, but great armies pay themselves."

"The only secret to prevent people speaking evil is to do no evil; but this secret is not infallible, although it ought to be so."

"Confederations, which make armies like pieces of mosaic, are useless."

"There is no condition which may not be made glorious, either by what is done or by what is suffered."

"There are few prisoners more closely guarded than princes."

"There is no salvation out of the Catholic Church; that is the only true oracle."

"Any gate through which one enters into a happy eternity is the triumphal gate."

"God rewards men more than they deserve, and punishes them less: we should imitate God."

THE END.

THE LIFE OF EDWARD IRVING, Minister of
the National Scotch Church, London. Illustrated by HIS JOUR-
NAL AND CORRESPONDENCE. By Mrs. OLIPHANT. SECOND EDITION,
REVISED. 2 vols. 8vo, with Portrait. 30s.

"We who read these memoirs must own to the nobility of Irving's character, the
grandeur of his aims, and the extent of his powers. His friend Carlyle bears this testimony to his worth:—'I call him, on the whole, the best man I have ever, after trial
enough, found in this world, or hope to find.' A character such as this is deserving of
study, and his life ought to be written. Mrs. Oliphant has undertaken the work, and
has produced a biography of considerable merit. The author fully understands her
hero, and sets forth the incidents of his career with the skill of a practised hand. The
book is a good book on a most interesting theme."—*Times.*

"Mrs. Oliphant's 'Life of Edward Irving' supplies a long-felt desideratum. It is
copious, earnest, and eloquent, carring the reader along, with something of the same
excited admiration and pathetic sensibility with which it is written. On every page
there is the impress of a large and masterly comprehension, and of a bold, fluent, and
poetic skill of portraiture. Irving as a man and as a pastor is not only fully sketched,
but exhibited with many broad, powerful, and life-like touches, which leave a strong
impression."—*Edinburgh Review.*

"We thank Mrs. Oliphant for her beautiful and pathetic narrative. Hers is a book
which few of any creed can read without some profit, and still fewer will close without
regret. It is saying much, in this case, to say that the biographer is worthy of the
man. * * * The journal which Irving kept is one of the most remarkable records that
was ever given to the public, and must be read by any who would form a just appreciation of his noble and simple character."—*Blackwood's Magazine.*

"A truly interesting and most affecting memoir Irving's life ought to have a
niche in every gallery of religious biography There are few lives that will be fuller
of instruction, interest, and consolation."—*Saturday Review.*

"A full detailed biography of Irving we have not seen till now. In Mrs. Oliphant's
volumes we trace the history, and mark the aspect, the joy, and grief, and conflict of
his life, as we have never before been able to do. Mrs. Oliphant's work is admirable,
presenting a most living, consistent, vivid picture of Irving."—*Macmillan's Mag.*

"We can allot Mrs. Oliphant no higher eulogy than that her work is worthy of him
whom it commemorates. She has contributed to our literature a work that will rank
among the best of biographies, one that may be placed by the side of Hanna's 'Life
of Chalmers,' and Stanley's 'Life of Arnold.'"—*Parthenon.*

"A highly instructive and profoundly interesting life of Edward Irving."—*Scotsman.*

ITALY UNDER VICTOR EMMANUEL. A
Personal Narrative. By COUNT CHARLES ARRIVABENE. 2 vols.
8vo, with charts, 30s.

"A bright and cheery book. A piece of history like the aspect and fortunes of the
land it describes so well, to freshen the memory and make glad the heart. Count
Arrivabene is a true artist. The sun shines on his page, and a youthful spirit glows in
his style. And then what a story he has to tell!—one that will interest the passions
of men and the sympathies of women to the end of time."—*Athenæum.*

"Count Arrivabene was singularly well qualified for the task he has here performed. His thorough mastery of our language enabled him to interpret his Italian
experiences to an English audience with a perspicuity which is rare even among our
own countrymen. His rank gave him access to the superior authorities everywhere,
and thus his information carries with it the stamp of authenticity, whilst his own natural
powers of observation and comment are considerable. He has produced a most important and stirring book. To say that it is interesting would be to express inade-
quately the absorbing power it exercises over the attention, and the excitement with
which it fills the mind."—*Daily News.*

"'Italy under Victor Emmanuel' merits, and will doubtless receive, considerable
attention. Under the writer's eyes were transacted the eventful scenes in which a
powerful nation was born out of a few petty states. The narrative is rapid, animated,
and breathlessly interesting."—*Cornhill Magazine.*

"Whoever wishes to gain an insight into the Italy of the present moment, and to
know what she is, what she has done, and what she has to do, should consult Count
Arrivabene's ample volumes, which are written in a style singularly vivid and
dramatic."—*Dickens's All the Year Round.*

LES MISÉRABLES. By VICTOR HUGO. THE
AUTHORIZED COPYRIGHT ENGLISH TRANSLATION.
SECOND EDITION. Complete in 3 vols. post 8vo. Price 31s. 6d.

"We think it will be seen on the whole that this work has something more than the beauties of an exquisite style or the word compelling power of a literary Zeus to recommend it to the tender care of a distant posterity; that in dealing with all the emotions, passions, doubts, fears, which go to make up our common humanity, M. Victor Hugo has stamped upon every page the hall-mark of genius and the loving patience and conscientious labour of a true artist. But the merits of Les Misérables do not merely consist in the conception of it as a whole, it abounds page after page with details of unequalled beauty."—*Quarterly Review.*

"'Les Misérables' is one of those rare works which have a strong personal interest in addition to their intrinsic importance. It is not merely the work of a truly great man, but it is his great and favourite work—the fruit of years of thought and labour. Victor Hugo is almost the only French imaginative writer of the present century who is entitled to be considered as a man of genius. He has wonderful poetical power, and he has the faculty, which hardly any other French novelist possesses, of drawing beautiful as well as striking pictures. Another feature for which Victor Hugo's book deserves high praise is its perfect purity. Any one who reads the Bible and Shakspeare may read 'Les Misérables.' The story is admirable, and is put together with unsurpassable art, care, life, and simplicity. Some of the characters are drawn with consummate skill."—*Daily News.*

"'Les Misérables' is a novel which, for development of character, ingenuity of construction, beauty of language, and absorbing interest of situation, is approached by very few. Having carefully examined Mr. Wraxall's translation of this celebrated work, we can conscientiously recommend it to the public as a perfectly faithful version, retaining, as nearly as the characteristic difference between the two languages admits of, all the spirit and point of the original. In its present form 'Les Misérables' stands a very fair chance of having as wide a sale as the French edition."—*Examiner.*

"There is much to admire in 'Les Misérables.' There are passages breathing the noblest spirit with a sustained loftiness of tone. There are others full of touching pathos. M. Hugo is one of the keenest observers and most powerful delineators of the human soul in all its various phases of emotion. Nor is it the fiercer gusts alone that he can portray. His range is wide, and he is equally masterly in analysing the calmer but more subtle currents which stir the heart to its very depths."—*Saturday Review.*

"A book replete with burning eloquence, with magnificent narrative, with astounding adventure."—*Daily Telegraph.*

THE PRIVATE DIARY OF RICHARD, DUKE
OF BUCKINGHAM AND CHANDOS, K.G. 3 vols. post 8vo, with Portrait, 31s. 6d.

Among others of the Duke of Buckingham's celebrated contemporaries and acquaintances, of whom anecdotes will be found in these volumes, are—George the Fourth; the Dukes of Clarence, Wellington, and Bedford; the Marquesses of Hertford and Lansdowne; the Earls of Shrewsbury and Westmoreland; Lords Grenville, Brougham, Errol, Yarborough, Arundel, Hardwick, Blessington, and Dalhousie; Sir Robert Peel; Mr. Canning; Ladies Shrewsbury, Westmoreland, Ponsonby, Errol, Brabazon, Howard, &c. Amongst the Royal and distinguished Foreigners are the Kings of the Two Sicilies and Bavaria, the Pope and the principal Cardinals, the Duke and Duchess of Modena, Maria Louisa, widow of Napoleon, Queen Hortense, Louis, Jerome and Lucien Bonaparte, Châteaubriand, and a host of the political, literary, and artistic celebrities of the period over which the Diary extends.

"A very amusing chronicle. That it will be read with curiosity we cannot doubt."—*Athenæum.*

"This Diary has intrinsic interest apart from the taste and intelligence of the writer. It abounds in anecdote."—*Examiner.*

THE CHURCH AND THE CHURCHES; or,
THE PAPACY AND THE TEMPORAL POWER. By Dr. DÖLLINGER. Translated, with the Author's permission, by WILLIAM BERNARD MAC CABE. 1 vol. 8vo, 15s.

"This volume is the most important contribution to the Roman question, and will long remain the greatest authority upon it. To theologians, the masterly review of all the existing churches and sects, as they bear upon the spiritual power, must be of im-

MESSRS. HURST AND BLACKETT'S
NEW WORKS—*Continued.*

ENGLISH WOMEN OF LETTERS. By JULIA
KAVANAGH, Author of "Nathalie," "Adéle," "French Women of
Letters," &c. 2 vols., 21s.

"This work of Miss Kavanagh's will be a pleasant contribution to the literature of
the times, and in raising a shrine to the merits of some of the leading English women of
literature, Miss Kavanagh has also associated her own name with theirs. The work
comprises a biography of each authoress (all women of renown in their day and genera-
tion), and an account and analysis of her principal novels. To this task Miss Kavanagh
has brought knowledge of her subject, delicacy of discrimination, industry, and a genial
humour, which makes her sketches pleasant to read."—*Athenæum.*

THE LIFE OF J. M. W. TURNER, R.A., from
Original Letters and Papers furnished by his Friends, and
Fellow Academicians. By WALTER THORNBURY. 2 vols. 8vo.
with Portraits and other Illustrations, 30s.

"Mr. Thornbury has had every possible advantage for the accomplishment of this
biography—a personal acquaintance with Turner, the advice of Mr. Ruskin, and the
ready assistance of all Turner's friends. Of the immense mass of materials brought
together Mr. Thornbury has made skilful use, and constructed an honest memorial of
the great painter. He has done his part ably. The artist will refer to these volumes
for authentic information regarding the great modern master and his works, and the student of life and manners will find in them a rich store of entertainment."—*Daily News.*

"Mr. Thornbury's work must not only be considered as the very best that he has
written, but as a valuable addition to our artistic biography. To the professional
student it will be especially interesting."—*Spectator.*

"Henceforward nobody can have any excuse for re-opening this subject. Mr. Thornbury has collected a mass of information larger in quantity and fuller in detail than Turner's uncommunicative character could have justified any one in expecting."—*Blackwood*

TRAVELS IN BRITISH COLUMBIA; with the
Narrative of a Yacht Voyage Round Vancouver's Island. By
Captain C. E. BARRETT LENNARD. 1 vol. 8vo.

"Captain Lennard describes British Columbia as a country in which the steady
emigrant may thrive whether as miner, manufacturer, or agriculturist. He was
two years on the Pacific Coast of the North American Continent, he made
numerous land excursions, with a visit to the Fraser River in Columbia. and to
New Westminster, the capital; he cruised round Vancouver's Island in a yacht,
and he became acquainted with many of the Indian tribes, few of which have
been familiarly known to Europe. We leave this lively and interesting volume to
the reader."—*Athenæum.*

"A most valuable accession to our Colonial literature. Captain Lennard gives a
vast amount of information respecting the two colonies, of that kind which an intending emigrant would be most glad to receive."—*Daily News.*

FEMALE LIFE IN PRISON. By a PRISON MA-
TRON. THIRD EDITION, WITH ADDITIONS. 2 vols., 21s.

"There are many obvious reasons why records of prison life should prove an attractive department of literature, though ordinarily they are more welcome than deserving
of encouragement, because they minister to the cravings of our curiosity only. The
present volumes have at least this higher pretension, that while they satiate our interest in pet murderesses and other prison monstrosities, they aim at affording us a
fuller view of the working of a retired and special department of State administration.
The authoress, who has herself been a prison matron, writes throughout with good
sense, good taste, and good feeling. The phenomena of female prison life which she
describes are most curious, and we consider her book to be as authentic as it is new in
the form and details of its information."—*The Times.*

"This book should have many readers among our social reformers of both sexes,
and few, if any, will close it without serious thought having been stirred by the
details and suggestions contained in it."—*Athenæum.*

"This is one of the most genuine books – probably the best woman's book of the
year. It is full of living interest. It is the genuine and simple utterance of experiences, interesting, touching, and useful to be known. It contains, besides the

MESSRS. HURST AND BLACKETT'S
NEW WORKS—*Continued.*

GREECE AND THE GREEKS. Being the Narrative of a Winter Residence and Summer Travel in Greece and its Islands. By FREDRIKA BREMER. Translated by MARY HOWITT. 2 vols., 21s.

" The best book of travels which this charming authoress has given to the public."—*Athenæum.*

" Miss Bremer has many things to tell of the king, the queen, and the country, that have a special interest at the present time."—*United Service Magazine.*

" Miss Bremer's work is full of the most vivid and picturesque descriptions of Greek life and scenery. It cannot fail to delight all into whose hands it may fall."—*Sun.*

DRIFTWOOD, SEAWEED, AND FALLEN LEAVES. By the Rev. JOHN CUMMING, D.D., F.R.S.E, printed on toned Paper. 2 vols., 21s.

MEMOIRS OF CHRISTINA, QUEEN OF SWEDEN. By HENRY WOODHEAD. 2 vols. with Portrait, 21s.

THIRTY YEARS' MUSICAL RECOLLEC-TIONS. By HENRY F. CHORLEY. 2 vols., with Portraits, 21s.

" Every page of these volumes offers pleasant reminiscences of some thirty years' experience. No one singer of merit, or pretension to it, no distinguished composer of the period, is without his or her portrait."—*Athenæum.*

THE LIFE AND CORRESPONDENCE OF AD-MIRAL SIR CHARLES NAPIER, K.C.B. From his Private Papers and Official Documents. By Major-General ELERS NAPIER. 2 vols. 8vo., with Portrait and Charts, 30s.

" A work of great interest, with much that is amusing for the general, and more that is instructive to the professional reader."—*Athenæum.*

FRENCH WOMEN OF LETTERS. By JULIA KAVANAGH, author of " Nathalie," " Adèle," &c. 2 vols., 21s.

" Miss Kavanagh's book is a very good one. It will obtain not only a popular success, but also a permanent place in the library. It covers ground new to most English readers Ten women—all very famous in their day—are taken as centres of literary history in successive periods; and in the story of their lives, still more in the analysis given of their works, we have the several stages of French life truly reflected."—*Examiner.*

TRAVELS IN THE HOLY LAND. By FRED-RIKA BREMER. Translated by MARY HOWITT. 2 vols., 21s.

" A good specimen of what travels should be—intelligent, unaffected, and giving exact impressions."—*Athenæum.*

THE OKAVANGO RIVER; A NARRATIVE OF TRAVEL, EXPLORATION, AND ADVENTURE. By CHARLES JOHN ANDERSSON, Author of " Lake Ngami." 1 vol., with Portrait and numerous Illustrations. 21s. bound.

" Mr. Andersson's book, from the number of well-told adventures, its rich fund of information, and spirited illustrations, will command a wide circle of readers. The interest of his story never flags for a moment."—*Athenæum.*

TRAVELS IN THE REGIONS OF THE

LODGE'S PEERAGE

AND BARONETAGE,

CORRECTED BY THE NOBILITY.

THE THIRTY-SECOND EDITION FOR 1863 IS NOW READY.

LODGE'S PEERAGE AND BARONETAGE is acknowledged to be the mos complete, as well as the most elegant, work of the kind. As an esta plished and authentic authority on all questions respecting the famil histories, honours, and connections of the titled aristocracy, no work ha ever stood so high. It is published under the especial patronage of He Majesty, and is annually corrected throughout, from the personal com munications of the Nobility. It is the only work of its class in which. *th type being kept constantly standing,* every correction is made in its prope place to the date of publication, an advantage which gives it supremac over all its competitors. Independently of its full and authentic informa tion respecting the existing Peers and Baronets of the realm, the mos edulous attention is given in its pages to the collateral branches ot th arious noble families, and the names of many thousand individuals ar ntroduced, which do not appear in other records of the titled classes. Fo ts authority, correctness, and facility of arrangement, and the beauty o ts typography and binding, the work is justly entitled to the place i ccupies on the tables of Her Majesty and the Nobility.

LIST OF THE PRINCIPAL CONTENTS.

Historical View of the Peerage.
arliamentary Roll of the House of Lords.
nglish, Scotch, and Irish Peers, in their orders of Precedence.
Alphabetical List of Peers of Great Britain and the United Kingdom, holding supe rior rank in the Scotch or Irish Peerage.
lphabetical List of Scotch and Irish Peers, bo'ding superior titles in the Peerage of Great Britain and the United Kingdom.
Collective List of Peers, in their order of Precedence.
able of Precedency among Men.
able of Precedency among Women.
he Queen and the Royal Family.
eers of the Blood Royal.
The Peerage, alphabetically arranged.
amilies of such Extinct Peers as have left Widows or Issue.
lphabetical List of the Surnames of all the Peers.

The Archbishops and Bishops of England Ireland, and the Colonies.
The Baronetage, alphabetically arranged.
Alphabetical List of Surnames assumed by members of Noble Families.
Alphabetical List of the Second Titles o Peers, usually borne by their Eldest Sons.
Alphabetical Index to the Daughters of Dukes, Marquises, and Earls, who, hav. ing married Commoners, retain the title of Lady before their own Christian and their Husbands' Surnames.
Alphabetical Index to the Daughters o' Viscounts and Barons, who. having mar ried Commoners, are styled Honourable Mrs.; and, in case of the husband being a Baronet or Knight, Honourable Lady Mottoes alphabetically arranged and trans lated.

" Lodge's Peerage must supersede all other works of the kind, for two reasons: first it i a better plan; and secondly, it is better executed. We can safely pronounce it to be th adiest, the most useful, and exactest of modern works on the subject."—*Spectator.*
" A work which corrects all errors of former works. It is a most useful publication."—*Times*
" As perfect a Peerage as we are ever likely to see published."—*Herald.*

Hurst and Blackett's Standard Library

OF CHEAP EDITIONS OF

POPULAR MODERN WORKS.

VOL I.—SAM SLICK'S NATURE & HUMAN NATURE.

" The first volume of Messrs. Hurst and Blackett's Standard Library of Cheap Editions of Popular Modern Works forms a very good beginning to what will doubtless be a very successful undertaking. 'Nature and Human Nature' is one of the best of Sam Slick's witty and humorous productions, and well entitled to the large circulation which it cannot fail to attain in its present convenient and cheap shape. The volume combines with the great recommendations of a clear bold type and good paper, the lesser, but still attractive merits, of being well illustrated and elegantly bound."—*Post.*

VOL. II.—JOHN HALIFAX, GENTLEMAN.

" This is a very good and a very interesting work. It is designed to trace the career from boyhood to age of a perfect man—a Christian gentleman, and it abounds in incident both well and highly wrought. Throughout it is conceived in a high spirit, and written with great ability. This cheap and handsome new edition is worthy to pass freely from hand to hand, as a gift-book in many households."—*Examiner.*

VOL. III.—THE CRESCENT AND THE CROSS.
BY ELIOT WARBURTON.

" Independent of its value as an original narrative, and its useful and interesting information, this work is remarkable for its reverent and serious spirit."—*Quarterly Review.*

VOL. IV.—NATHALIE. BY JULIA KAVANAGH.

" ' Nathalie' is Miss Kavanagh's best imaginative effort. Its manner is gracious and attractive. Its matter is good."— *Athenæum.*

VOL. V.—A WOMAN'S THOUGHTS ABOUT WOMEN.
BY THE AUTHOR OF " JOHN HALIFAX, GENTLEMAN."

" A book of sound counsel. It is one of the most sensible works of its kind, well written, true-hearted, and altogether practical."—*Examiner.*

VOL. VI.—ADAM GRAEME OF MOSSGRAY.
BY THE AUTHOR OF " MARGARET MAITLAND."

" ' Adam Graeme' is a story awakening genuine emotions of interest and delight by its admirable pictures of Scottish life and scenery."—*Post.*

VOL. VII.—SAM SLICK'S WISE SAWS
AND MODERN INSTANCES.

" The best of all Judge Haliburton's admirable works. It is one of the pleasantest books we ever read, and we earnestly recommend it."—*Standard.*

VOL VIII.—CARDINAL WISEMAN'S POPES.

" A picturesque book on Rome and its ecclesiastical sovereigns."—*Athenæum.*

VOL. IX.—A LIFE FOR A LIFE.
BY THE AUTHOR OF " JOHN HALIFAX, GENTLEMAN."

" In ' A Life for a Life ' the author is fortunate in a good subject, and she has produced a work of strong effect."—*Athenæum.*

VOL. X.—THE OLD COURT SUBURB. BY LEIGH HUNT.

" A delightful book; that will be welcome to all readers, and most welcome to those who have a love for the best kinds of reading."—*Examiner.*

VOL. XI.—MARGARET AND HER BRIDESMAIDS.

MISTRESS AND MAID. By the Author o
"JOHN HALIFAX, GENTLEMAN." 2 vols.

"All lovers of a good novel will hail with delight another of Miss Mulock's charmin fictions. In 'Mistress and Maid,' the characters, like all Miss Mulock's, are abl sketched and well supported. The gentle elder sister, so resigned for herself, so care for the sister child she has nurtured with all a mother's loving care; the fretful beau whose ill-temper is the cankerworm of the little household; the energetic, stron hearted, loving, and loveable Hilary, the breadwinner of the family; and the good ang of the house, the serving maid of the sisters, Elizabeth Hand, are so naturally an vividly portrayed, that they seem like old acquaintances.—*John Bull.*

"Never lies the truth of that noble aphorism, 'one touch of nature makes the who world kin,' been more forcibly verified than in this very charming story."—*Messenger*

A PRODIGAL SON. By DUTTON COOK, Autho
of "Paul Foster's Daughter." 3 vols.

"'A PRODIGAL SON' will find many admirers among readers of works of fictio There are new characters in the book, and the plot is good."—*Post.*

DAVID ELGINBROD. By GEORGE MACDONAL
M.A. Author of "Within and Without," "Phantastes," &c. 3 vol

A POINT OF HONOUR. By the Author of "Th
Morals of May Fair," &c. 2 vols.

SLAVES OF THE RING; or, Before and Aftei
By the Author of "Grandmother's Money," &c. 3 vols.

"A very good story. The reader cannot but feel interested in the loves, the joys, ar sorrows of 'The Slaves of the Ring.' It is no small praise to say that the present ta possesses in almost every respect the good qualities of the author's previous works." *Observer.* "These volumes well sustain the author's reputation."—*John Bull.*

THE MAROON. By CAPTAIN MAYNE REID, Autho
of "The Rifle Rangers," &c. 3 vols.

"Capt. Reid has the advantage of being able to add what may be called person experience to a more than ordinary happy power of description, 'The Maroon' wi rank among Capt. Mayne Reid's most popular books."—*Athenæum.*

THE LADIES OF LOVEL-LEIGH. By th
Author of "Margaret and her Bridesmaids," &c. 3 vols.

"The author of this interesting tale has not now for the first time proved to tl world her extraordinary power in delineating the affections. The lesson is one impressive force."—*Daily News,* "A very pleasant novel."—*Press.*

MARION LESLIE. By the Rev. P. BEATON. 3 vol
"This story is a very good one, and is told with great power. The descriptions Scottish life are drawn with a very graphic pen."—*John Bull.*

JOHN ARNOLD. By the Author of "Mathe\
Paxton." 3 vols.

OWEN: A WAIF. By the Author of "Hig
Church" and "No Church." 3 vols.

"There is a generous heart speaking with power through the tale of 'Owen,' and t characters are sketched with genuine humour."—*Examiner.*

CAN WRONG BE RIGHT? By Mrs. S. C. HAL
"This excellent and interesting story is the best Mrs. Hall has written."—*Athenæu*

THE LAST OF THE MORTIMERS. By th
Author of "Margaret Maitland," &c. 3 vols.

"A charming book—simple, quaint, and fresh.—*Athenæum.*